CLAIMING YOUR
POWER

THROUGH
ASTROLOGY

A SPIRITUAL WORKBOOK

Emily Klintworth

Schiffer Publishing Ltd®

4880 Lower Valley Road • Atglen, PA 19310

Acknowledgments

Before I wrote a book, I used to breeze right through these sections at the beginning, thinking how could there be so many people to thank and dedicate a book to? And now that I've written a book, I get it! There are so many beautiful spirits that help influence and bring these visions to life. They are the midwives of this world helping to create the wonderful and powerful things we call books.

An endless thanks to Dinah and Schiffer Publishing—their dedication to creating and printing the highest quality books inspires me. As the world evolves, we will never lose the need to learn and grow through books. Their gift to the world is remembering the root of why authors write and bringing that vision to life in every aspect. Thank you for allowing me into the Schiffer family. Any author who is lucky enough to work with Schiffer has received the most powerful gift, a place where their visions can be treated with respect and nurtured to their full potential.

I also want to thank my family and specifically my sister, who with a glass of red wine, flew through my book and confidently completed every exercise. Ali, I'll never forget when I came over to your home and you marched your copy right over to me. You sat down and started to tell me all about what you had uncovered while reading the book. When you asked that I please return it when I was done making my edits, I was deeply validated. Thank you for your feedback and insights. You helped strengthen this concept and provided me with direction—this vision evolved because of you.

I also want to thank a very special friend, Cassandra Clegg. When I was a retail manager she found her way into my life as a holiday employee. When I later brought her back as a permanent team member, she humbly credited it to her new love of "chanting" and told me she put it out into the Universe—she wanted to work with me again. I am so happy that I can now call you a friend and explore the spiritual aspects of life with you. Your love, encouragement, and belief in my gift helped me overcome the voice in my head. Thank you for diligently reading my book, marking it up with post-its, and highlighting every line that spoke to your spirit—for each note and highlight gave me courage to speak my truth. Thank you.

It would be crazy for me not to mention the other HUGE part of what makes this book possible: the Natal Chart Navigator. Thanks to the programming genius of Allen Edwall, my vision and concept became a reality. He is a talented, generous, and knowledgeable soul—what a blessing to have found him. Also a sincere thanks to the creativity and web brilliance of Janet with Creative Siren; she is a true collaborator and visionary. Her design and direction for my website has paved a way for what's to come. Thank you both for creating the other half of my book—the very part that makes this spiritual workbook possible.

I also want to thank Linda Howe and her beautiful gift to the world, evolving the method of accessing the Akashic Record. Years ago, I chose to go to her for a reading. She declared to me that this life I was living was about bridging two things: power and creativity. She energetically assisted in clearing a pathway for me to realize this goal. Through her training in the Akashic Record, I become more confident in offering readings and exploring and sharing my intuitive gifts. A sincere thank you for being a guide of light during the more difficult portion of this journey.

I have one more person to thank. I want to thank *you*, the reader. Thank you for being brave enough to open your mind to this ancient art of astrological interpretation. Thank you for picking up this book, purchasing it, and supporting me as a writer. It is my sincere hope that this book repays you three-fold and more, opening you up to new levels of consciousness and validating who you truly are: spirit in a human body.

I DEDICATE THIS BOOK TO
TWO VERY IMPORTANT PEOPLE IN MY LIFE.

First, my dear mentor, teacher, and friend, Nancy Murdock-Gulliksen. I tell her often that she has impacted my life in profound ways—without her wisdom and guidance, I would have sifted through the vast astrological concepts lost and without direction. She has erased years of trial and error that I may have endured if not for her astrological proficiency and talent. Words can never do justice to the gratitude, appreciation, and deep love I feel for her. Due to her thirty-plus years working as a professional astrologer, she has given me a gift that I feel deeply blessed to have received. Many of the insights and concepts you will explore in this book were birthed through her teachings and guidance. I want to provide her with a very big thank you for taking me on as a student. Being an astrologer isn't necessarily an easy path, but it is one that I am so thankful to have found, and I'm forever blessed to have found her as my teacher.

The second person I dedicate this book to is my husband, Adam. I have been blown away by his unconditional support, love, and encouragement. I am beyond thrilled with our ever-evolving relationship and the beautiful gifts it has brought into our lives. He has truly gone above and beyond in helping me make my dreams a reality, and I realize not many husbands would be all for their wife deciding one day to become an astrologer. Thank you for reading every draft and doing every exercise in this book. Thank you for watching our kids the moment you got done with work so that I could run down to the basement and bring this vision to life. Without you, I would not laugh so very much or find so much joy surrounding me every day. Our children are blessed to have you as their father; endlessly making them giggle and squirm. Thank you for teaching me that laying down roots is a good thing—it is truly the most powerful way to grow.

"A child is born on that day and at that hour
when the celestial rays are in mathematical
harmony with his individual karma."
—SRI YUKTESWAR GIRI

Contents

Foreword

The Consciousness Revolution is well underway with exciting new ideas, approaches, and assumptions leading to new results. For the first time in thousands of years, secular people like you and I have the opportunity to explore and cultivate our own spiritual awakening. Fortunately, for every type of human being alive, there are corresponding strategies for spiritual growth. In this time of global awakening to the realization of our Oneness, we can trust that all roads are leading us home. Each of us is challenged to find our own Path, embrace it, and stride it with dignity.

The lens I employ is the Akashic Record, using the Pathway Prayer Process© to access this soul level dimension of consciousness. For me and countless others, it is ideal as an infinite spiritual resource for personal empowerment and transformation. The Record is the story of our soul through time and space, exploring a variety of incarnational experiences. Every lifetime, we have the chance to know and love ourselves in ever-increasing ways as we grow in conscious awareness of the Unity of all our souls.

Astrology is a complementary discipline for enjoying a more conscious connection with our soul and insight into our purposes and intentions in this life. Our astrological imprint in the Natal Chart is the blueprint of our soul in this specific incarnation. As we grow through life—surfing progressions, solar returns, and planetary tensions of every conceivable variety—the essential truth of who we are, and who the others in our life are, is revealed.

The book you hold in your hand is likely to be the key to your next step. Emily's work is aligned with the great Aquarian Age Imperative, where each individual is responsible for their own spiritual authority. You have access to a loving guide and teacher in her. She offers inspired wisdom and practical exercises designed to awaken you to the marvels of who you are and the magnificent life you are living.

Emily provides you with the opportunity of the Age—spiritual experience rather than religious ideals. Know that your teacher is highly qualified with astrological skills, intuition, compassion, and spiritual wisdom. Trust that you have arrived at the door of your next stage of growth and empowerment.

And, like all the other stars in the galaxy, Shine! Shine! Shine!

—Linda Howe
Award-winning author* and spiritual teacher

---

* *How to Read the Akashic Records* (2009, Sounds True)
Healing Through the Akashic Records (2011, Sounds True)
Discover Your Soul's Path Through the Akashic Records (2015, Hay House)

Introduction

You are about to embark on a journey, one where you will be provided with the opportunity to step outside yourself—to view your life through the lens of the cosmos. Although this book uses astrology as a tool, it is has not been created to teach you everything there is to know about this ancient art (although you will certainly learn along the way). There is no need to memorize or pore over facts in this book. This is a spiritual workbook, and there is nothing you need to know about astrology prior to embarking on this journey.

The book has been divided into two sections: Exploring Your Natal Chart and Aligning with the Cosmos. The first section will assist you in deepening your understanding of why you are here, your life purpose, and your unique spiritual makeup. The second section builds on the first, and introduces the predictive nature of astrology. Here you will gain valuable insight into the cyclical nature of astrology (and life) by exploring career, marriage, children, and much, much more!

The chapters have been designed specifically to enable you to approach this complex topic from a new angle, each chapter building on the one before it. For this reason, I recommend following them sequentially and not jumping back and forth based on subject matter. Trust me, you may want the insight of a particular chapter, but if you haven't built the fundamentals, you risk the possibility of not being able to absorb the concept as deeply as you could have.

Accompanying each chapter is a handcrafted, artistically designed exercise—get ready to put your pen/pencil to the paper! You are absolutely meant to write in this book and make it your own. By completing each of the exercises, you will be able to apply each of the concepts to your chart and, by doing so, invite that new awareness into your life. Through this process you will begin to learn how to claim your power—to trust your instincts and believe in your life purpose.

Before you get started, there is one very important thing you must do. You must download your free Natal Chart Navigator from www.absolutelyastrology.com to complete the exercises. The Natal Chart Navigator has been created specifically for you and this book. It is extremely easy to read and must be used to complete the exercises (side note: my husband has completed every exercise and declared to me that if he could do it, anyone could!). On the website, you will need to input three vital pieces of information: date of birth, time of birth, and location of birth. Please note: birth time is extremely important. Yes, we astrologers are always going on about birth time for a very important reason! Even four minutes can make a huge impact in your chart. *If* there is no way for you to gather that bit of information, an alternative chart can be created, but it may be slightly less accurate. Please only choose that route if you have exhausted all other measures.

My advice to anyone who is about to begin this astrological journey is to be patient and to open yourself up to the endless gifts, insights, and advice that this art can provide. Although I wish I could take credit for everything in this book, I simply cannot. I am a vessel that is only capable of showing you the way and guiding you along. Every insight, moment of clarity, and breakthrough you receive along the way is uniquely *you*.

Before you begin, please visit
www.absolutelyastrology.com
to download your free
Natal Chart Navigator
and print it out for reference
during the exercises.

There are sample exercises available for reference in the back of the book to support you on this spiritual journey. (Be sure to use them as you complete your worksheets.)

If you anticipate that you will want to complete the exercises for a child, parent, or loved one, I highly recommend copying the blank exercises before filling them out.

SECTION 1
EXPLORING
YOUR
NATAL CHART

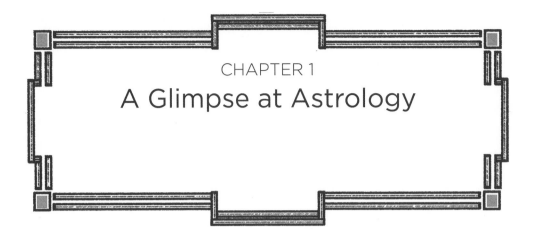

CHAPTER 1

A Glimpse at Astrology

POWER PLAN

○ Discover what a Natal Chart is and an introduction to the Zodiac, Planets, and Houses
○ Explore the 12 Signs of the Zodiac through Element and Mode
○ Understand how the planets affect the Houses based on their distribution in your chart

When I was a young girl, I had an experience so intriguing that it inevitably shaped my entire childhood. One night, I awoke and saw a spirit at the foot of my bed. I was startled, as anyone would be, and from that moment on, I knew that I was a spirit in a human body. You can imagine the curiosity that would develop in such a young mind. I immediately found myself interested in anything "new age." I soon became obsessed with a tiny, little esoteric shop nestled just off the main road in my hometown. This obsession grew, and I never felt a need to conceal it. I was always very different, honest, and straightforward. I had to be, as I knew that there was a lot more going on in this world and I needed to find out what.

I couldn't have known at the time, but that experience became the seed of my greatest curiosity: what are we all doing here? So when the gift of my intuition grew, I welcomed it with open arms. One of my earliest visions was of a very simple concept: just as we vacation here on

Earth, it was a "vacation" from the other side that had brought us here. When we plan a vacation, we pick a specific destination and duration of time we will be spending there. We decide who will be going with us and what activities we want to include. There is evidence of all of these decisions that we make: tickets we purchased for our travel, itineraries mapping out how we would like our vacations to unfold, etc.

It shouldn't be surprising then that we planned for this incarnation. And of course, it shouldn't be surprising at all that there is evidence and an "itinerary" for how our lives are going to unfold. The Astrological Natal Chart (Birth Chart) is this itinerary. This chart is a map of the heavens at the moment of your birth. It depicts the exact location of each planet in what is known as the Tropical Zodiac. The position of the planets is recorded, and then it is pulled into a circle with 12 Astrological Houses. Your time of birth is used as the "tuning fork" to draw that data into your chart. The 1st astrological house is calculated based on the exact degree of the sign rising at the moment of your birth.

The calendar year was originally created to mark the Sun's apparent journey (known as the ecliptic) through the fixed constellations in the sky and subsequently its journey through the zodiac. The Earth's orbit around the Sun creates four seasonal changes that we all know: summer, fall, winter, and spring. As the Earth moves around its orbit, the two points where its axis causes it to be straight with the Sun are referred to as the Equinoxes (occurring in March and September). The other two points where the Earth reaches its maximum angle compared to the Sun are called the Solstices (occurring in June and December). The Tropical Zodiac, which we use in this book, is reflective of the seasonal changes and cycles. The art of astrology arose due to the validity of aligning with these celestial movements. Through trial and error this ancient language developed, and over time it transformed into a sacred tool used to assist man in reaching new levels of consciousness. Although it takes 365 days for the Sun to complete its journey, the zodiac uses 360° because it was easier and neater to work with.

Whenever you have read your "horoscope" in a newspaper or magazine, your "sign" is actually the zodiac sign that the Sun was in at the moment of your birth. If you have known yourself as a "Libra," the Sun was in the sign of Libra on the day that you were born. Sun signs proved much easier to calculate than the other planet locations (the date of birth being all you needed) and thus it became an easy way to deliver quick and somewhat relevant astrological perspective. In the Tropical Zodiac, the start of the Sun's journey through the zodiac starts on the spring Equinox each year and marks the starting point of the first sign in the zodiac, Aries. This projected zodiac circle is 360° and broken down into 12 sections/signs, each 30°. The Sun starts its journey, in the first sign of the zodiac, Aries, and continues through each sign as follows: Taurus, Gemini, Cancer, Leo, Virgo, Libra, Scorpio, Sagittarius, Capricorn, Aquarius, and Pisces.

Originally, the Ascendant (the sign rising at the moment of your birth) was the most prominent component of your Natal Chart, but due to the difficulty in calculating it, mainstream astrology focused on the Sun Sign/Birth Sign. One of the gifts of the technological revolution that we are experiencing is that what once took astrologers hours to calculate by hand, now only takes minutes. Accessing this information has become extraordinarily easy and it is providing us with a pivotal way to dive deeper than ever into the cosmic potential we each hold within.

Although the zodiac is technically an imaginary circle projected out from the Earth, it reflects 12 energy patterns and is an integral part of the language astrologers use to interpret the unseen forces of this world. Each "energy" pattern is a combination of specific characteristics, traits, and approaches to life. Astrology is a language, and it is the combination of the planets, their location in the zodiac, and their location in the astrological houses (based on time of birth) that allows us to interpret and provide valuable insights. The astrological houses are also broken up into 12 segments just like the signs, but they are a method astrologers developed to predict in what area of your life these "energies" would be expressed. The houses and signs, although similar, represent two different things in astrology—the signs represent the energy expression (the how) and the houses express where it is showing up in your earthly experience (the where).

When you are working with the Astrological Natal/Birth Chart, you are looking specifically at what zodiac sign your planets appeared to be in at the moment of your birth (this changes how the celestial rays come into alignment with your being). There are many planets (Sun, although a star, is referred to as a planet) that astrologers will utilize to help gain insight about your life. In this book we will be working with the following: Sun, Moon, Mercury, Venus, Mars, Jupiter, Saturn, Uranus, Neptune, and Pluto. The Moon, which is a satellite of Earth, and Pluto, which is a dwarf planet, will also be referred to as planets. Additionally, there are "sensitive points" that have historically proven to hold insightful information: Ascendant, South Moon Node, North Moon Node, and Part of Fortune.

The planets in astrology are telling us "what" is happening, the Signs tell us "how" it is happening, and the houses tell us "where" it is happening. For instance, let's say we have the Moon in the sign of Libra in the 7th House. The Moon refers to the emotional and instinctual self (the "what") and is expressing itself through the Sign of Libra (the "how") in House 7, which rules partnerships (the "where"). As we explore the planets, signs, and houses further, you will discover that Libra represents the archetype of The Peacemaker. Based on the location of the Moon, we would say it indicates that your natural instinct (Moon) in relationships (House 7) is peace seeking (Libra), and you avoid conflicts whenever possible. Don't worry if this feels a little overwhelming. This book is designed to guide you through each concept while providing an exercise to help you fully understand what it means for you in your life right now.

The houses are the main road map and can be used to help guide you in your life. Just as you would pull out a map (or check the Internet) to figure out where a specific city is or the best route to take, you can utilize the houses in the same way. They are telling you exactly where certain energy dynamics are showing up in your life. It's crazy to think that there was a time when all I had to find a friend's house was a beat-up map, or some scribbled directions on a piece of paper. Now, I have a navigation system on my phone that speaks to me as I'm driving. As far as I'm concerned, using your Natal Chart for spiritual navigation is just as viable as the map app on the phone—it has the potential to make things happen faster and more accurately in your life. It's there, so why not take advantage of this sacred tool? Why not use it to help you get the most out of your life?

Your basic map is composed of what houses these planets occupy in your chart. For instance, House 9 is about travel, education, and literature. I have a Power Cluster of planets in this house (a total of 4 planets) and have always been drawn to all three of those things my entire life. When it came to travel, sometimes I wanted to explore and to feel alive. Other times, I craved solitude and a time to connect with my inner being. A Power Cluster (3 or more planets in close proximity to one another) will always indicate a focused energy for you in this life. When numerous planets gather together in a chart, just like the dynamics of a group, their power grows stronger and more apparent. There will be an exercise at the end of this chapter to help you assess if you have any Power Clusters present in your chart. If you do not discover a Power Cluster within your chart, this is an indication that you choose to spread your energy in multiple directions. In this case, you have chosen a "jack of all trades" approach to your life experience.

I love to travel and since the houses show the "where" of how the energy will be expressed, my Power Cluster in House 9 was inevitably going to draw me to the areas of life ruled by that house: education, travel, and writing. One of my favorite trips happened when I spent my final semester of college abroad in London. I had formed an extremely tight bond with my roommate, Marie, even though we were polar opposites. I was the hippy proclaiming in my Research Studies class that I wanted to assess the Dalai Lama through past-life readings. She was prim and pressed in her polo T-shirt holding her Louis Vuitton bag, which she lovingly called, "Louis." Together we decided on our long Easter weekend that we would go on a trip. We had been given some free tickets for early enrollment and decided we would use them to go to Paris.

The whole city was bustling due to the holiday weekend and we quickly discovered the flaw in our plan. All the hotels were booked solid, as were the hostels. So we decided to leave Paris and go somewhere else where we could get a room. The woman at the ticket counter suggested a town called Lille and off we went. It was a wonderful trip filled with funny mishaps, and it took us over a day to figure out how to reverse the car. For the first twenty-four hours, Marie would jump out of the car and push it so that we could reverse. Finally, I became desperate enough to take action (I originally was trying to avoid being the stereotypical American). I spotted a nice couple in the parking lot of our hotel and desperately asked, "*Parlez-vous Anglais*?" When they responded, "*Oui*" I blurted out, "How do I reverse the car?"

The truth was I wanted to go to Lourdes because I had heard about the various sightings of the Virgin Mary. Marie wasn't as keen on this idea and wanted a completely different travel experience. Discovering how you would approach travel and how it would play a role in your life can all be explored in your Natal Chart. This is how my desire to travel was inevitably going to be different than Marie's. Each of us has a specific sign ruling each of the 12 houses. Typically, each house has two signs present and both approaches (signs) work together to create the energy that will most likely be experienced in those specific areas of your life.

My 9th House has the energy of Libra and Scorpio. I was largely drawn to travel for my desire to connect with others (Libra) and my deep spiritual needs to find more answers (Scorpio). Marie's 9th House is ruled by Aquarius (always looking to learn) and Pisces (always seeking to please). Should I be surprised then that Marie woke at eight a.m. each morning to "frolic" and explore the city and its history? Or that when we were on that trip in France, she had to go to mass because she didn't want to make her mother upset? Given the insights from her chart, I'm not surprised at all.

Together, we will explore numerous concepts of Astrological Natal Chart interpretation and work with them piece-by-piece. By breaking each concept down and applying the information immediately to your Natal Chart, you will be able to understand how these concepts reflect in your life. The goal is not to teach you everything there is to know about astrology, but to rather provide tools for self-exploration so that you can begin to gain insight and validation into who you are and why you are here.

Each chapter will include a power plan to allow you to prepare for the information and concepts that will be delivered. At the end of each chapter, there will be an exercise for you to complete and apply to your individual Natal Chart. It may take you a little bit longer in the beginning to complete the exercises, so please be patient with yourself. You will get the hang of things quickly, but you must learn the basics of the signs, houses, and planets (don't worry, no memorization—just a basic understanding of their function). As you fill out your blank exercises, you can refer to the sample worksheets at the back of the book as examples. (I'm with you every step of the way—I have completed each exercise myself and these are the examples you will be looking at). Please use the example exercises for reference if you feel confused or if you would like to double check that you are completing everything accurately.

A Natal Chart Navigator is free to download at www.absolutelyastrology.com. This Navigator has been uniquely designed to work with the exercises in this book. In order for this Navigator to be generated, you will need to input your birth data. Please make sure that you have your date of birth, time of birth, and location of birth ready. I highly recommend locating your birth certificate to verify your birth time as it proves to be the most accurate method for obtaining this information. As you complete the exercises, you will notice that it will reference the various tables of this Natal Chart Navigator (be sure to read through the brief summary above each table for easier navigation prior to getting started).

You may discover that you have an affinity for astrology and want to learn more throughout this book. Please know that there are many detailed astrology books out there for further knowledge. Book recommendations are made in the reference section for further exploration if you so desire. My advice to those who do become inspired to pursue the art of astrological interpretation: be patient with yourself as you begin to learn this ancient art—it is a life-long pursuit.

As you've learned, it is the combinations of the planets, signs, and houses that enable an individual to provide astrological interpretation. It's time now, to dive into the planets and learn how they operate in each of the 12 signs of the zodiac. Each sign can be broken down by Element and Mode. There are four elements: Fire, Earth, Air, and Water and each element has three modes: Cardinal, Fixed, and Mutable. This makes for 12 combinations (4 elements, and 3 modes) and corresponds to the 12 signs of the zodiac. This means that each sign contains the traits and characteristics of the mode and element that are contained within it. This is why someone with their Sun in Taurus (a fixed earth sign) will have a different makeup than someone with their Sun in Sagittarius (a mutable fire sign).

By looking at the dominant element and mode for your chart in this first exercise, we can begin to piece together significant patterns and characteristics about who you are. We determine the dominant element and mode by evaluating your natal planet locations in the zodiac. Below lists each of the elements and their general characteristics and tendencies:

FIRE

Very in tune with the physical body and the "fight or flight" sensations. This is someone who can generate many ideas in a seemingly short amount of time. This person is spontaneous and ready to act. With this much energy, it is important to keep it channeled and moving forward. This energy needs to feel alive. It is the energy of the natural leaders. If you are not focusing this energy, it can back up and cause extreme physical exhaustion. The response style of individuals with dominant fire in their chart is instinctual. This element corresponds with the Signs: Aries, Leo, and Sagittarius, and the Houses: 1, 5, 9.

EARTH

This is a common-sense energy, working hard to earn the right to play hard. This energy seeks not only purpose through work, but to enjoy the fruits of its labor. Ruling the five senses, this energy comes to life through sight, touch, sound, smell,

and taste. This energy needs to take advantage of the luxuries of life or will easily become demotivated. The response style of individuals with dominant earth in their chart is receptive. This element corresponds with the Signs: Taurus, Virgo, and Capricorn, and the Houses: 2, 6, 10.

AIR

This energy is highly intellectual and constantly seeking new abstract ideas to explore. It is an energy that hops from idea to idea and has chameleon-like capabilities. Having the ability to see the broad perspective, it can often overlook the smaller details. It has a hard time following through and can often procrastinate decision-making or deadlines. The response style of individuals with dominant air in their chart is intellectual. This element corresponds with the Signs: Gemini, Libra, and Aquarius and the Houses: 3, 7, 11.

WATER

This is the most intuitive and emotional element in the zodiac. Water seeks to connect with all that it can, through the densest of material or energy. This element needs to experience the sensations of human connection and growth through relationships. It is often empathetic, and if not cautious can take on others' troubles as their own. The response style of individuals with dominant water in their chart is emotional. This element corresponds with the Signs: Cancer, Scorpio and Pisces, and the Houses: 4, 8, 12.

Your dominant element will begin to reveal to you the general tendencies you have with your approach to life. The 4 Elements are a powerful way that you can begin to explore and understand the inner nature of yourself and those closest to you. Every individual has their own unique combination of the elements and this is very reflective of the inner world and nature of the individual. For instance, someone with a lot of Fire energy in their chart will most likely be extremely passionate, creative, and constantly hungry for life experiences (and also prone to aggression). On the flip side, someone without any Fire in their chart may experience a lack of those qualities. It is safe to say that this is the "default" setting of the inner world, and that as we grow and evolve, we learn to express these qualities in a way that allow us to function as efficiently as possible in this world. If you have a tie between your dominant elements, you would be expressing the traits of the dominants equally more than the other elements.

It's important to recognize that we all have the 4 Elements in us, just at varying degrees. I discovered the accuracy of using this particular tool in my readings because, in almost all cases, the effects of the dominant elements or deficiencies were acutely felt by the individual. Just the mere recognition of why they were experiencing an "extreme" allowed a deep sense of relief to flood into their consciousness.

It can be a very fun process to understand why we magnetize (or repel) to various individuals we encounter throughout our lives. This is one of the first tools I teach to those interested in going deeper into astrology for personal or business applications. For instance, there are many individuals who either have that dominant Element or even a deficiency in one of the four Elements: Fire, Earth, Air, and Water. If you experience an extreme dominant energy or a deficiency, having the opportunity to receive tips for managing dominant Elements or activating deficiencies can literally be life-altering. To learn more about this topic, you can sign up for my free 4 Elements of Spirit Workshop at www. absolutelyatrology.com/freeworkshop.

We can further explore these tendencies by determining your most dominant mode: Cardinal, Fixed, or Mutable. As we discovered earlier, the 12 signs of the zodiac are composed of the four elements: Fire, Earth, Air, and Water, which are being expressed through the three modes: Cardinal, Fixed, and Mutable.

This means that there will be a Cardinal Fire (Aries), Fixed Fire (Leo), and Mutable Fire (Sagittarius); a Cardinal Earth (Capricorn), Fixed Earth (Taurus), and Mutable Earth (Virgo); a Cardinal Air (Libra), Fixed Air (Aquarius), and Mutable Air (Gemini); and lastly, a Cardinal Water (Cancer), Fixed Water (Scorpio), and Mutable Water (Pisces). The easiest way to think of the modes is as a representation of the natural evolution of the human experience: birth/ beginning (Cardinal), life/focus (Fixed), death/ transformation (Mutable). Keep this in mind as you read on about each of the modes:

CARDINAL

This is the initiating energy in the zodiac. It is "full steam ahead" and ready to act. It enjoys new adventures and new projects (it should, because it probably thought of them). Not afraid of challenges and both physically and intellectually strong.

FIXED

This is the deeply committed energy always looking to see a project through. This may not be the energy that creates the projects or initiates them, but it surely is the energy that sees it to fruition. The energy does not walk away—once it commits, it commits.

MUTABLE

This is the flexible energy, bending with the wind. This energy embraces change as an inevitable part of life and isn't afraid of what it may bring. It is neither the initiator energy nor the energy that finds it necessary to see things through to the end. Because of this, this energy can often have a hard time laying down roots.

One of my clients and friend, Leigh, has 7 planets in the Cardinal mode and 3 in Mutable. During her first reading, when we discussed that specific dynamic, she felt incredibly validated. I told her that there would be so much in her calling for change and adventure (7 planets in Cardinal). But when it came down to that actually happening, she would have anxiety of seeing it through (3 planets in Mutable). She told me that she had been trying to explain this to her cousin who wouldn't believe her. Her cousin told her, "No one who wanted to do all those things, could have all that anxiety about them." I immediately replied, "All you've got to do is look to the stars." That is, the truth is always offering us a new perspective on who we really are.

Once you determine your dominant element and mode, the second exercise for this chapter will allow you to determine if you have any Power Clusters in your chart. Remember, a Power Cluster always indicates an intense focused energy in a specific area of life—this can often be seen from an early age. If you have three or more planets in a house, you have a Power Cluster in your chart (I'm sure you've felt it). That specific area of life will hold much importance for you, but the energetic validation you receive by seeing it in your chart—truly priceless.

Through the initial chapters of this spiritual workbook our focus is on laying down the foundation for all the information, insights, and moments of clarity that are to come. As you begin to familiarize yourself with this new language, be patient, kind, and open to the insights that are making their way into your life. Know that each chapter marks movement forward—the journey is only just beginning.

MODES

Cardinal Fire (Aries)
Fixed Fire (Leo)
Mutable Fire (Sagittarius);

Cardinal Earth (Capricorn)
Fixed Earth (Taurus)
Mutable Earth (Virgo);

Cardinal Air (Libra)
Fixed Air (Aquarius)
Mutable Air (Gemini);

Cardinal Water (Cancer)
Fixed Water (Scorpio)
Mutable Water (Pisces).

Start Your Exercises!
ELEMENT & MODE EXPLORATION
POWER CLUSTERS & HOUSE EXPLORATION

Taking your first step on this spiritual journey, you discover your dominant Element: Fire, Earth, Air, or Water and your dominant Mode: Cardinal, Fixed, or Mutable.

ELEMENT & MODE EXPLORATION

WATER

FIRE

AIR

EARTH

FIRE

♈ **ARIES**
MODE: CARDINAL

♌ **LEO**
MODE: FIXED

♐ **SAGITTARIUS**
MODE: MUTABLE

EARTH

♉ **TAURUS**
MODE: FIXED

♍ **VIRGO**
MODE: MUTABLE

♑ **CAPRICORN**
MODE: CARDINAL

AIR

♊ **GEMINI**
MODE: MUTABLE

♎ **LIBRA**
MODE: CARDINAL

♒ **AQUARIUS**
MODE: FIXED

WATER

♋ **CANCER**
MODE: CARDINAL

♏ **SCORPIO**
MODE: FIXED

♓ **PISCES**
MODE: MUTABLE

CARDINAL | FIXED | MUTABLE

STRONGEST ELEMENT:

STRONGEST MODE:

TALLY THE MODES IN THE BOXES ABOVE FOR EACH PLANET

EXERCISE
Element & Mode Exploration

Each sign in the zodiac is the combination of an element and mode. In the four rectangles below the circle, the signs have been sorted by element: Fire, Earth, Air, and Water. Each mode for the specific sign is also listed just below its name: Cardinal, Fixed, and Mutable. Follow the steps to complete this first exercise. There is a sample worksheet for you to reference as you complete each exercise located in the Appendix (the page number is referenced at the top of each worksheet).

STEP 1:
The circle on the worksheet is divided into quadrants. Each quadrant represents an element: Fire, Earth, Air, and Water.
The 4 blocks below the element and mode circle show the elements with their appropriate signs.

1. Using Table 1 in your Natal Chart Navigator, look at each planet in column 1 and its matching sign in column 2.

2. Using the table, look at the 4 element boxes on the worksheet to see which planet should be written in each quadrant of the circle. (For example: if your Sun is in Pisces, the boxes below the circle show Pisces in the Water element box. Write Sun in the Water quadrant of the large circle.) This shows where each sign was when you were born.

3. Once you look up each sign to discover the element and mode activated and have written the planet into the element circle at the top, tally the mode in the bottom boxes. (The modes are shown in the element boxes below each sign. Use the key box below to check off each planet as you go.

☐ sun ☐ jupiter
☐ moon ☐ saturn
☐ mercury ☐ uranus
☐ venus ☐ neptune
☐ mars ☐ pluto
☐ ascendant

STEP 2:
1. Look to see which element and mode is strongest in your chart by adding up the totals.

2. Once they have been discovered, write them into the circles below entitled Strongest Element and Strongest Mode. You can read more about the elements/modes in this chapter for further insight.

EXERCISE
Power Clusters
& House Exploration

The circle to the right shows each of the 12 Astrological Houses in Astrology. Within the circle are three words that describe the dynamics at play in each house. Please ensure you have your Natal Chart Navigator ready to complete the following steps.

STEP 1:

Now it's time to write the planet/points of your Natal Chart into the Astrological Houses.

Look to Table 1 in your Natal Chart Navigator to determine the house location for each planet in column 4. Utilize the Planet/Points Key to keep track as you enter each Planet/Point into the chart.

* Please note that you will not enter the Ascendant

STEP 2:

If you have three or more planets in a house, you have a "Power Cluster." This is an indication of a strong focused energy in that area of your life. The words on the innermost portion of the circle reflect what areas of your life this focused energy will be affecting.

If you identified a power cluster in your chart, write "Power Cluster" in the blank innermost circle along with the three words listed for that house. If you did not discover a power cluster in your chart, write "jack of all trades" into the middle circle.

Discover your approach to life through the distribution of the planets in the Astrological Houses. Do you have a Power Cluster? Or have you chosen a jack-of-all-trades approach?

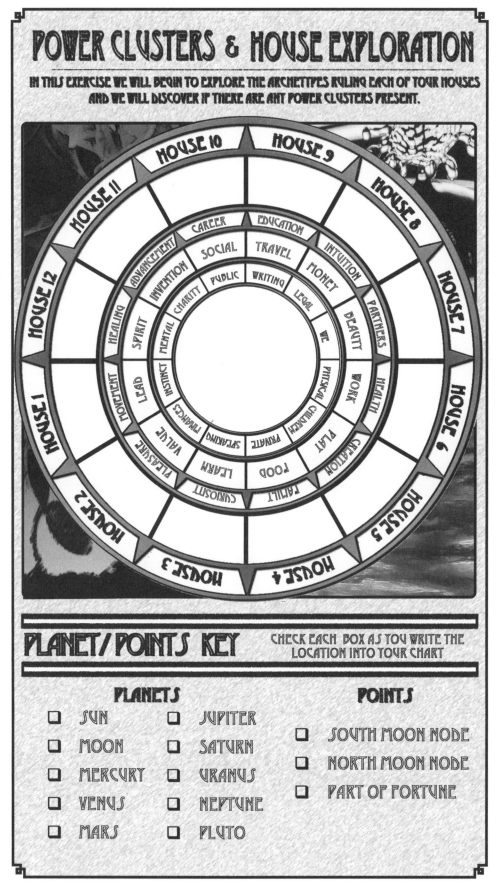

POWER CLUSTERS & HOUSE EXPLORATION

IN THIS EXERCISE WE WILL BEGIN TO EXPLORE THE ARCHETYPES RULING EACH OF YOUR HOUSES AND WE WILL DISCOVER IF THERE ARE ANY POWER CLUSTERS PRESENT.

PLANET/POINTS KEY

CHECK EACH BOX AS YOU WRITE THE LOCATION INTO YOUR CHART

PLANETS

- ☐ SUN
- ☐ MOON
- ☐ MERCURY
- ☐ VENUS
- ☐ MARS
- ☐ JUPITER
- ☐ SATURN
- ☐ URANUS
- ☐ NEPTUNE
- ☐ PLUTO

POINTS

- ☐ SOUTH MOON NODE
- ☐ NORTH MOON NODE
- ☐ PART OF FORTUNE

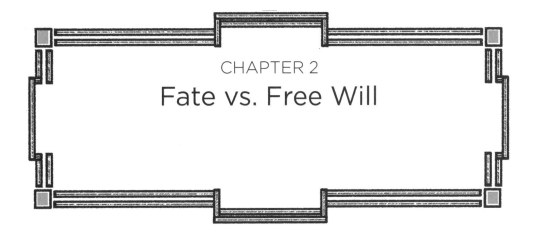

CHAPTER 2
Fate vs. Free Will

POWER PLAN

△ Discover how fate and free will work together in your life
△ Learn what areas of your life have the fates involved
△ Learn what areas of your life rely mostly on creation through free will

When I was in college, my friend Annie lent me a book by Shirley MacLaine called *The Camino*. It was one of those books that immediately connected with my inner being. I couldn't put it down. I was entranced by her words and wanted to experience walking this spiritual pilgrimage across northern Spain. In my journal, I wrote a list of things I wanted to accomplish: live in England, earn my MA in creative writing, and walk The Camino. Years later, when cleaning out a dusty bin at my parents house for what felt like the millionth time, I found that journal and that list—I had accomplished it all. It's funny how easy these things feel when we have already done them. We forget the distance we had from our dreams when they were in the seedling stage of our unconscious.

All three of those things happened together; I applied and was accepted to an MA program in England, moved there, and then walked The Camino. It didn't come together overnight, however. Getting past the first stage in the application process for the MA program was

indeed fated for me. What I chose to do in the next stage, however, can only be described as 100% free will. Bath Spa University had requested a phone interview, and I knew myself well enough to know I would be more successful in person. So I decided that I would fly to England for that interview—100% free will in getting there, 100% fate in how it developed from there.

I stayed in London with a friend and took the bus to Bath where I stayed at a traditional English-style bed and breakfast. I felt so alive that morning, knowing that I had chosen to take a chance on myself. I rode the bus to the university and silently explored the grounds while passing time until my interview. I eventually found myself in a room, sitting directly across from the director of the English Department, Richard, and one of the head poets of the program, Tim Liardet.

Richard and Tim asked me many questions during this interview, one being, "What poets have inspired you?" I answered honestly, "I'm not well read in poetry, but I will dedicate myself to learning and reading the major poets before I would start here. I think that my fresh perspective and me being so new to all this would be a nice new energy for the program." I could tell they didn't know what to make of me. I hadn't read a lot of poetry and in the past had written for fun and the therapeutic benefit. I had been honest and I could tell that while Tim respected my honesty, Richard began to doubt I was what they were looking for. I decided, as I always do, that the truth would set me on my right path. So I chose to go with that thought and when the opportunity arose, I proclaimed, "I'm a psychic." I could tell in that moment, that my future writing mentor, Tim, grew curious as to whom this strange young American girl was.

Tim quoted one of my poems I had submitted, "envy grew like ivy on my pale limbs." He asked, "How did you come up with this, if you aren't well read in poetry?" I again answered with the truth, "I had a vision of it. I saw it and I wrote it." Tim saw me as the peculiar, honest, different creature that I was. When I left that day, I knew the truth of it all—Tim was fated to be in that room. It came down to Tim versus Richard on whether or not they would choose to accept me into the program. I waited for about a week before hearing back. I was accepted, thanks to the curious poet who had the power to demand my entry into the program.

So off I embarked on another adventure! Two of those beautiful dreams were being fulfilled from my list and I innocently walked right into the third. I struggled so much in the beginning of my program (probably to Richard's delight of proving Tim wrong), but I kept telling my tutor that I would have a breakthrough moment. I declared that I would be walking a pilgrimage called The Camino across Spain. I told him it would change the course of my whole life and my writing. I remember him looking at me with such concern, wondering how I could believe that to be true. I told him bluntly and honestly that he would soon see…

And he did. Something happened as I walked The Camino. Every day was a blessing carved out to my spirit and helped me let go of a somewhat painful past. At the end of each long and grueling day on the path, I wrote while nestled in my bunk.

And as my visions became stronger, my words became more precise. Each step I took was one step closer to figuring out who I was.

When I came back, the poetry poured out of me. The lines were crisp and clean. The words could paint the images the same way I saw them in my mind and my tutor was flabbergasted. I sat there with a group of five to eight poems and he couldn't believe it. He said my "voice" had changed and the level of my work had tripled. I wish for one minute I could understand his experience of me in that moment—the underdog making her voice heard (a pattern repeated a vast amount of times in my life).

Our paths are an interwoven web of free will and fate. Some of the greatest gifts of our lives are fated, but require free-will action to accept them into our lives. Just as I had decided to take that plane to England and to walk that path down The Camino, free will and fate had worked together.

I had a vision of this concept: Fate versus free will. I imagined that I was in the sky staring down on Earth. There was a beautiful path throughout an immense dense forest. The path came to points where it diverged and sometimes three paths emerged out of just that one. Then intermittently and at different times, they converged right back on to that same path. Always moving forward and covering ground, but sometimes on completely different terrain. This was my visual representation of how fate and free will worked hand in hand.

On the other side, we chart these different paths and options. We are not limited by linear time there, so it is very easy for us to visualize three roads leading to the same culminating event. There isn't just one road leading us towards our greater purpose here on Earth. There are many different roads, shortcuts, and detours. Our free will is choosing each and every road we go down. And yet, as if by magic, they do converge again and again—bringing us back to our one same truth, helping us honor the flow and rhythm of our lives.

Being able to identify the areas of your life that you left 100% to free will can allow you to begin to claim more personal power in your life. There are two easy ways to explore this concept in your chart, and we will do both in the exercises at the end of this chapter. If you divide your chart in half vertically, you can gain a general sense of the fates involved in your life. The more planets on the left-hand side of your chart indicate free will and the more planets on the right-hand side indicate fate.

My brother has 9 planets on the right side of his chart, indicating that fate would play a leading role in how his life would unfold. He is eight years older than me, and I've always looked up to him fondly, admiring his kind spirit and quick humor. His first job after college involved painting our three-story Victorian home for some fast cash. After the summer was over, my parents honored "tough love" and kicked him out. He then took a job at the Board of Trade and moved to a small run-down apartment in Chicago. He worked there for a few months and then fate called. A college friend working as a trader in Germany contacted him and offered him an opportunity of a lifetime. My brother eagerly accepted. I went with my parents to the airport where I watched my brother throw a duffel bag over his shoulder and board an airplane headed for Frankfurt.

He didn't speak a word of German, but it didn't matter. His charm and ease of character has always made it incredibly easy for him to make friends and he became an outstanding options trader. While humbly crediting his early love of video games to his success, he made in minutes what many make in hours or days. The fates then provided another opportunity for him, and he was cast in a television show called *High School Reunion*. I clearly remember during a trip to Costa Rica when he was recognized on the plane. As I watched his path unfold, I just saw him rolling with the punches. I knew it was an unusual tale. I wasn't surprised then to later find that his chart showed how fate would play a role, but I also saw where fate didn't show up, where he had to use free will to bring into his experience that which he was seeking.

We can always look a little deeper in astrology and here we can further explore the dynamics of fate versus free will in our chart by the houses. Any of the houses you see where you have no planets, indicate that those areas of your life will largely be left up to you. For instance, if you have the 7th house empty (like my brother), you may not have picked the specific person you would marry in this life. This doesn't mean that it is all completely up to chance, though, because you would have picked in general how you would approach love through the placement of Venus in your chart. You also would have picked some basic characteristics about the love you were looking to experience based on the sign ruling that house. The main thing you can take away from a house with no planets is that you wanted whatever decisions you made to be rooted in this incarnation—you wanted free will to reign.

When working with the free will energy of your chart, I have personally found it extremely beneficial to focus in on the details of what you are looking to experience. By cleaning up your energy field and feelings toward a subject, it can allow the law of attraction to assist you in bringing into your life that which you are seeking. As we evolve our consciousness as a species, more and more will be left to free will. But for now, we experience the combination of both.

Start Your Exercise!
FATE AND FREE WILL

Fate and free will practice their wild tango in the undercurrent of your life—
discover which one is taking the lead.

EXERCISE
Fate vs. Free Will

NOW IT IS TIME TO DISCOVER THE INFLUENCES OF FATE AND FREE WILL IN YOUR LIFE. REMEMBER, THERE WILL BE FATED MOMENTS THROUGHOUT YOUR ENTIRE LIFE. HOW YOU REACT AND THE ROAD YOU CHOOSE EACH TIME IS ULTIMATELY UP TO YOU. CHOOSE WISELY

STEP 1:
Looking back to the last exercise, determine the number of planets and sensitive points in each house.

STEP 2:
Write each number into the inner circle and the correct house on the worksheet detailing the discovery of the influences of fate and free will in your life.

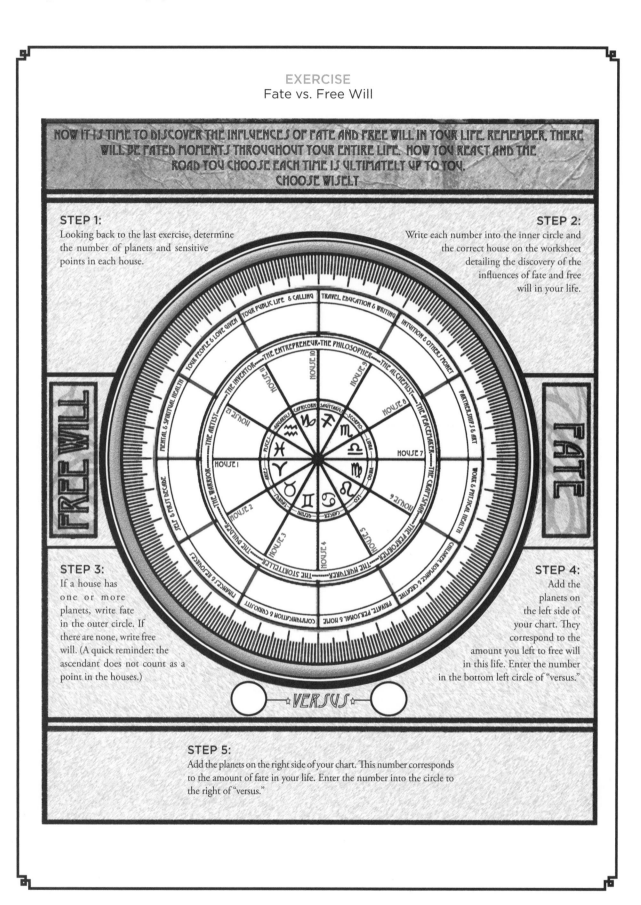

STEP 3:
If a house has one or more planets, write fate in the outer circle. If there are none, write free will. (A quick reminder: the ascendant does not count as a point in the houses.)

STEP 4:
Add the planets on the left side of your chart. They correspond to the amount you left to free will in this life. Enter the number in the bottom left circle of "versus."

STEP 5:
Add the planets on the right side of your chart. This number corresponds to the amount of fate in your life. Enter the number into the circle to the right of "versus."

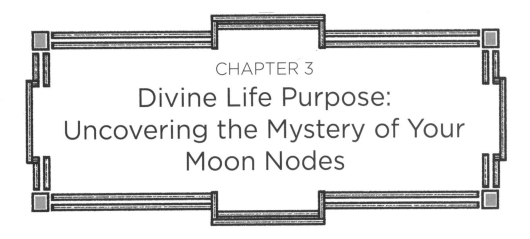

POWER PLAN

△ Understand the concept of your True North and your internal compass within
△ Learn what energy patterns your spirit explored in past lives
△ Discover what energy patterns your spirit wants to explore in this life

One of the most remarkable things in this world is to plant a seed and watch it grow. You place it in the soil, water it, and make sure it has plenty of sunlight. You wait and wait until one day you see a little sprout push through the soil and reach for the sun. Scientists are only now discovering how the seed, in complete darkness, knows which way to grow. And it truly is remarkable—that internal compass within the seed. Tests show that if you flip the seed upside down in a cup after it has sprouted, it will in fact redirect its roots. It knows its True North. Wouldn't it be amazing if you knew yours?

There is a compass inside you. You can view it in your Natal Chart. You may have felt its pull, but it's possible with all the stress in this world that you haven't heard it—it could be as slight as a faint whisper. Just like the seed in the darkness of the soil that grows through instinct, so can you. The answer to discovering this direction lies in the location of your Moon Nodes of your chart. Your True North in this life is where your North Moon Node is located. Your roots (where you have been

and what supports you as you push forward) are where you will find your South Moon Node.

One of the first things an astrologer must do before interpreting a chart is determine the spiritual direction. This becomes the necessary backdrop for every other piece of information that is interpreted—it is the key to unlocking the full potential of a chart. The Moon Nodes, just like the planets, will be located in a specific house and sign within your chart. To understand the basic pull of your life we can look to the Moon Nodes to begin to uncover your deeper purpose. Our first step in interpreting the Moon Nodes is to identify the quadrant they each are located in, and with that knowledge, we determine the current running through your life experience.

Many concepts of astrology will reference the quadrants of your Natal Chart. This is because each of the four quadrants represent a very powerful collective energy that personifies the three signs of each quadrant. There are four quadrants, which can be visualized by taking a circle (your Natal Chart) and dividing it both horizontally and vertically.

The first quadrant appears at the bottom lower left portion of the circle, and it correlates to Houses 1-3 and the signs Aries, Taurus, and Gemini. The second quadrant appears in the lower right, and it correlates to Houses 4-6 and the signs Cancer, Leo, and Virgo. The third quadrant appears in the upper right portion of the circle, and it correlates with Houses 7-9 and the signs Libra, Scorpio, and Sagittarius. The final fourth quadrant is in the upper left portion of the circle, and it correlates to Houses 10-12 and the signs Capricorn, Aquarius, and Pisces.

The quadrant in which your South Moon Node is located shows you where the bulk of your past life energy has been focused. This often translates into a practiced, behavioral part of your personality and affects you in a very powerful way (it's what you've known to do in the past and often a pattern you have a hard time letting go of). Because this energy (South Node) represents an energy pattern that you have experienced through multiple past lives, the area activated by the South Node typically represents that which comes easy to you. The tricky thing is, we must remember that our goal in this life is to utilize the old energy patterns and not fall back on them—we must push forward and still learn, grow, and evolve.

The North Moon Node always represents where we are going and the new energy pattern we want to experience. By following this direction, we are then able to live a life that allows us to come into "full bloom." It represents our very own True North.

How the planets are pulled into the Natal Chart is not random and requires delicate calculation to ensure accuracy. There are multiple house systems (calculations) that astrologers use to determine these locations. For the concepts explored in this book, I recommend the Koch house system—this is what was used to calculate how the signs of the zodiac pull into the houses in your Natal Chart Navigator. The 1st House is always calculated by the rising at the moment of your birth sign. That sign and degree are known as your Rising sign/Ascendant—this changes one degree every four minutes in the day

(passing through the entire zodiac in twenty-four hours).

You can think of the Natal Chart as a clock with midnight representing the lowermost portion of the circle and noon representing the uppermost portion. If you were born at night when the Sun was down, your Sun will be in one of the houses below the horizon line (Houses 1-6). If you were born when the Sun was up, your Sun will be in the top portion of the circle (Houses 7-12). Depending on the time you were born, your Sun will be in a specific house to reflect that time in your Natal Chart. Keep in mind that the directions are reversed in the Natal Chart—the top of the chart represents South and the lower portion represents North. This is why House 1 marks the Ascendant/Rising sign because it represents the direction East, where the Sun rises. The start of the first House correlates to 6 a.m. and if you were born around that time, you will most likely have your Sun and Ascendant in the exact same sign.

Seeing the intricacy of the house calculations for your chart, you are now aware of how important birth time is. It is definitely worth digging around or ordering a new copy of your birth certificate to verify this information. As we explore the energy patterns from your past lives, we begin to form an even deeper understanding of the importance the quadrants play. Each quadrant represents the collective energy of the signs and houses within it and becomes the foundation for how we decipher the information. Astrologers form interpretive sentences by putting together the planets, signs, and houses. It is like learning a foreign language, but the good news is that I will be your interpreter and guide for this entire spiritual workbook and journey.

Let's take a look at the different quadrants so that we can begin to familiarize ourselves with their energy and insights. Remember, the South Node indicates where you have been and the North Node indicates where you are going. Your South and North Node will always be opposite one another in your Natal Chart.

Following you will find an interpretation for the quadrants and a short note for the South and North Nodes.

The Four Quadrants

QUADRANT	HOUSES	SIGNS
1 (lower left)	1-3	Aries, Taurus, Gemini
2 (lower right)	4-6	Cancer, Leo, Virgo
3 (upper right)	7-9	Libra, Scorpio, Sagittarius
4 (upper left)	10-12	Capricorn, Aquarius, Pisces.

QUADRANT 1 (Lower Left):
Houses: 1-3
Signs: Aries, Taurus, Gemini

This quadrant represents individuation from the collective and a firm grasp as an individual entity. The Aries energy brings a strong, powerful, and independent nature and activates the fight/flight sensation. In fact, those with a Node in this quadrant will most likely be very in tune with the signals from the physical body. Taurus brings a love of beauty and enjoyment—pushing this energy to explore the gifts of this world through the senses. Gemini activates the internal thinker and provides a pivotal need to learn how to express oneself through verbal communication. Together, these signs activate the pattern of discovering your spirit through the, "I." If you have either Node in this location, you will want to feel like you can take care of yourself and this will be very important for you in this life. Read on to see how the North and South Nodes react in this quadrant.

South Node: If this is where your South Node is located, it indicates that through many past lives you ultimately were responsible for taking care of yourself. You've been the sole provider and were responsible for meeting the needs of yourself and your family. This energy is ingrained in you and as you push towards your North Node in Quadrant 3, you may find it difficult to let go of your independent nature. You are beginning to learn how to function and grow through relationships and may not always know how to behave.

North Node: If your North Node is located in this quadrant—it is time for you to learn how to put yourself first. This quadrant represents survival energy, and if this is where your North Node is located, it will be incredibly important for you to secure your own resources in this life. You may even want a separate bank account and private access to money to ensure you feel like you can take care of yourself. In many past lives, you put others needs before your own and you were the afterthought—its time to let that go. It's time to embrace your inner guide and live a life of purpose to discover who you really are.

QUADRANT 2 (Lower Right):
Houses: 4-6
Signs: Cancer, Leo, Virgo

The collective energy of this quadrant is reflective of family and associating with a tribe. Cancer brings an emotional connection to others and a need to feel loved and supported. It is complimented by Leo's playful and childlike approach—calling you to a creative expression in any way that inspires you. Virgo adds its energy by helping to create order, efficiency, and purpose. If you have a Node in this quadrant, you will always have a deep pull to create a powerful and safe personal space in this life. The energy of this quadrant relates to the private, personal, family, and home. There will be a call within you to honor the sacred space and ritual, living for the moments and extending yourself to your immediate family—your chosen tribe. Read on to see how the North and South Nodes react in this quadrant.

South Node: If your South Node is located in this quadrant, you are being pulled into the public arena during this life, but you will require a stable foundation and home. You will never lose sight of the importance of family and your chosen tribe, but your career and calling have great importance as well. This life is about balance and discovering how you can honor your tribe and family, while you still embark on an equal journey of your career calling and service to the public.

North Node: If your North Node is located in this quadrant, you are being pulled to create a family and spend a great deal of time in your home. You have built leadership skills through your past lives and will find it easy to manage and take a prominent role in your work. The career part of your life will be of high focus, but if that is all you seek, you will always feel a sense of emptiness. This is because you are being called into this quadrant and the private, personal, family, and home. This can express on multiple levels, but is often an indication that you will work out of your home, have children, or have a work environment that is very family oriented.

QUADRANT 3 (Upper Right):
Houses: 7-9
Signs: Libra, Scorpio and Sagittarius

The collective energy of this quadrant centers on relationships and personal growth. Libra is a peace-seeking energy that thrives off the one-on-one connection. Scorpio fuels the physical need to connect, and Sagittarius provides you with a quest to know yourself through others and knowledge. If you have a Node in this quadrant, much of what you learn in this life is derived from your relationships. This could refer to romantic relationships, marriage, friendships, and even business partnerships (you'll have plenty to experience). If you have either of your Nodes in this quadrant, it indicates that relationships will play a central part to your life. It is very important to understand if this is a new or old pattern by which Node is located here—your experience of relationships is dramatically affected by this information. Read on to see how the North and South Nodes react in this quadrant.

South Node: If your South Node is located in this quadrant, you have practiced the art of relationships in many past lives. You have learned how to put the

needs of others first and are able to care deeply for the lives of those around you. This life will push you to actively move into the "I" and to learn how to express yourself as an individual. You may find that you are constantly in relationships (it's an old habit), but the world will constantly remind you that the most important relationship for you in this life—is the one you have with yourself.

North Node: If your North Node is located in this quadrant, you are beginning to learn how to function in relationships and to put the needs of others before your own. This is a brand new pattern for you and you may find that your behaviors don't always create the relationships your heart is seeking. This falls back onto the many lives you had of being a sole provider for yourself—it is time to let go and seek to honor another. You will learn that as you put the needs of another first and release your need to be right or in charge, all things will fall into a more harmonious expression. Focus not on how you can get someone to love you, but rather on how you can love another.

QUADRANT 4 (Upper Left):
Houses: 10-12
Signs: Capricorn, Aquarius, and Pisces

This quadrant represents our movement forward as a collective—as a whole and as a society. Capricorn brings a hard-working career focus and the need to have purpose at all times. Aquarius activates the intellect and makes you hungry for solutions and a need to move the world forward. Pisces adds an element of empathy and art—helping you to connect with others and support one another through a creative expression. If you have a Node in this quadrant, you will have a natural leadership presence in this world. You will find it easier to talk to the masses and to enable others to find their path. There is a sense of responsibility to the world when one of your Nodes sits in this quadrant. You are meant to be before the public. You are meant to make a significant impact on others.

South Node: If your South Node is in this quadrant, you are a natural leader and can easily influence those around you. You find it a very easy thing to walk into a room and change the energy (you have spent many past lives learning this skill). If, however, you only pursue this portion of your journey—you will be left with a small portion of your heart that feels empty. This is because you are here to learn how to form a tribe and family of your own. Do not get distracted by what comes easily.

North Node: If your North Node is in this quadrant you are being called before the public and there will be a part of your spirit that knows this. You are learning how to be a leader and how to influence others in this world—you will not be satisfied until you make an impact. Your career will be of high importance to you and it will be at the forefront of your life (this is good). Individuals that hear this call do their part to assist society to evolve and provide great inspiration to the world. It will be very important for you to plan and dedicate time to your family/tribe, but this is not to distract you from your duty to the public—you must do both.

THE MOON NODES

The Moon Nodes are there in your chart, offering you this wisdom. When we harness the power of this pull and direction, we will be pulled by destiny. Things that you never could imagine happening will often begin to show up and support you in your life. By locating the quadrants of your South and North Moon Node, you have determined the current carrying your life. We can gather even more information by looking at the specific house that the Node was located in.

Following is a list of the Houses. I recommend highlighting or circling the house for both your South and North Moon Node (reference your Natal Chart Navigator). Just next to South Moon Node you can write, "Where I've been." Just next to North Moon Node you can write, "Where I'm going."

_____ House 1: Physical Self & Identity
_____ House 2: Finances & Values
_____ House 3: Communication & Siblings
_____ House 4: Family & Private
_____ House 5: Children & Creative Expression
_____ House 6: Work & Daily Habits
_____ House 7: Marriage & Partnerships
_____ House 8: Spiritual Transformation & Cycle of Life
_____ House 9: Education, Writing & Travel
_____ House 10: Career & Calling
_____ House 11: Invention & Humanitarian
_____ House 12: Art & Soul Connection

The incredible life of Mother Teresa shows the power of following this internal compass. Her South Node, where the bulk of her past life energy has been, is located in the 11th House (Quadrant 4). This house is the House of Social Change and Humanitarian Works. The inventive energy of this house pushes us to move forward and to break through social barriers. Mother Teresa came into this life with her roots firmly planted in that knowing—she had to have spent many lives working within that energy to be able to apply it the way that she did. Her True North pointed her to take her gifts and move them into a new direction (Quadrant 2).

She said that she knew from a young age that she would devote her life to religious works. Harnessing the energy of her Moon Node, she followed that calling. She served as a teacher in Calcutta for almost twenty years, and then she was appointed to head mistress. But it was a "call within a call" according to her that had her leave the convent and tend to the poor. She said, "I was to leave the convent and help the poor while living among them. It was an order. To fail would have been to break the faith."[1]

At the time of her death, she had created homes for orphaned children, homes for people with HIV or Aids, leper colonies, and hospices for the terminally ill.[2] She created a space for people to live—she created homes. It isn't surprising then that her True North (North Node) was in House 5, in the quadrant relating to the private, personal, and home. She created homes in the best way she knew how. This shows the power and the beauty that can come from harnessing the energy of your South Node. Using it to help us establish the energy that our True North is taking us to.

In the last chapter, we discovered the nature of free will and fate in our lives. We can look now to the quadrants where our North and South Nodes are located. If you have planets in these quadrants, you can begin to piece together more information about your plans for this incarnation. Ideally—you have many planets in the quadrant of your North Node and this indicates that you have chosen to have many fated events align you with your life's current. If, however, you discover you have no planets in the quadrant of your North Node, you have not planned for many fated events—this indicates that you wanted this alignment to come through free will in this life. You can easily flip back to the second exercise in chapter 1 to determine the impact of fate and free will on your Moon Nodes.

Mother Teresa had two powerful planets in the quadrant of her North Node: Moon and Saturn. This indicates that she had outside forces helping to align her with her life's current—she chose to have certain fated events help set her to her right path. As you will learn throughout this book, there are multiple ways to interpret information in a chart. One of the ways we could interpret this information is based on the Moon as representative of the Mother/Female influence and Saturn as the representation of the authority figure in her life. In this case, we would know that there was something inherent in the relationships that she had with the authority figures in her life that would push her to embrace her calling.

There have been many moments and periods in my life when I did the exact opposite of following the pull of my Moon Nodes (and did I feel it!). Imagine your life purpose as a beautiful winding cobblestone path. Looking out from this path, you can see the trees, plants, and life hugging the road. We are allowed to explore that terrain and add new dimensions of our choosing to our life path through free will, but as we explore, we will learn that just beyond sight from our path there is a fence. This fence keeps us from moving so far away from our path that we wouldn't have a chance at getting back. That is where I have spent a few long stretches of this life—running into that fence over and over, not understanding why I felt so stagnant or uninspired. For some reason, I would have it in my mind that I could break through the fence or climb over it to get to the other side (like the harder I worked or the worse I felt, the more I was accomplishing). So there I would be, running harder and at different angles, trying to jump high enough so that I could catch the top with my hand. The truth is, living in alignment with your life purpose will always feel expansive to you, even if it's scary and unknown.

This is of course all part of the free will aspect of our journey here. The "fence" is a boundary we set up for ourselves—all we have to do is listen. You are never so far from your path that you can't simply turn around and get right back on course. Your Moon Nodes provide you with one of the most powerful tools for spiritual development. You now know your intentions from the other side and by consciously choosing to embrace this current, you open your life up to reaching its full potential.

Start Your Exercise!
DIVINE LIFE PURPOSE

Determine the karmic imprint of your past lives and the spiritual direction you are taking in your current incarnation.

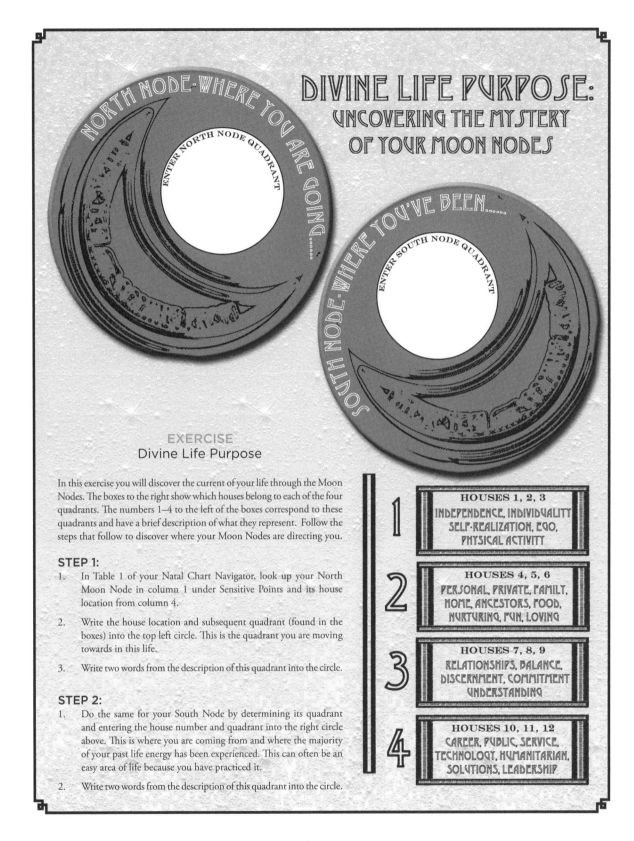

DIVINE LIFE PURPOSE:
UNCOVERING THE MYSTERY OF YOUR MOON NODES

NORTH NODE-WHERE YOU ARE GOING......

ENTER NORTH NODE QUADRANT

SOUTH NODE-WHERE YOU'VE BEEN......

ENTER SOUTH NODE QUADRANT

EXERCISE
Divine Life Purpose

In this exercise you will discover the current of your life through the Moon Nodes. The boxes to the right show which houses belong to each of the four quadrants. The numbers 1–4 to the left of the boxes correspond to these quadrants and have a brief description of what they represent. Follow the steps that follow to discover where your Moon Nodes are directing you.

STEP 1:

1. In Table 1 of your Natal Chart Navigator, look up your North Moon Node in column 1 under Sensitive Points and its house location from column 4.

2. Write the house location and subsequent quadrant (found in the boxes) into the top left circle. This is the quadrant you are moving towards in this life.

3. Write two words from the description of this quadrant into the circle.

STEP 2:

1. Do the same for your South Node by determining its quadrant and entering the house number and quadrant into the right circle above. This is where you are coming from and where the majority of your past life energy has been experienced. This can often be an easy area of life because you have practiced it.

2. Write two words from the description of this quadrant into the circle.

1
HOUSES 1, 2, 3
INDEPENDENCE, INDIVIDUALITY SELF-REALIZATION, EGO, PHYSICAL ACTIVITY

2
HOUSES 4, 5, 6
PERSONAL, PRIVATE, FAMILY, HOME, ANCESTORS, FOOD, NURTURING, FUN, LOVING

3
HOUSES 7, 8, 9
RELATIONSHIPS, BALANCE, DISCERNMENT, COMMITMENT UNDERSTANDING

4
HOUSES 10, 11, 12
CAREER, PUBLIC, SERVICE, TECHNOLOGY, HUMANITARIAN, SOLUTIONS, LEADERSHIP

Endnotes

1. "Mother Teresa—Questions and Answers," last modified Web. 4 Oct. 2015, www.nobelprize.org/nobel_prizes/peace/laureates/1979/teresa-faq.html.
2. Ibid.

CHAPTER 4
The Signs and Their Archetypes

POWER PLAN

△ Learn how to use the archetypes to understand the 12 Signs of the Zodiac
△ Explore the dynamics the inner planets play in shaping your personality
△ Create an archetype summary to explore your personality's purpose in this life

As a Mother, I have been able to witness a spiritual phenomenon through the birth of my two children. From the moment they began to grow in my belly, I have seen their spirits come into this life with very specific personalities. How incredibly unique and specific everything was about them from their very first breath. I was affirmed that the moment we enter this world, we come equipped with the personality that will accompany us on our entire life journey. From whether we are outgoing or introverted, all the way to how we cope with stress, it's all already ingrained. As life continues to shape us, the core of who we are never truly changes; it merely evolves. We are in a constant state of spiritual evolution and this personality is your life-long tool for processing and understanding your earthly experience.

Most everyone has become familiar with his or her "sign" and in many cases this would have provided some accurate interpretation. This is because the Sun represents our individual

expression in life—it is how we choose to shine. However, after you read about your Sun Sign, although you may have felt somewhat validated, you most likely felt like something was still missing. This is because something very important *was* missing—the location of the planet in the houses. If you have known yourself as a Libra, there is another sign that was also activated by the time of your birth. Each astrological house activates a specific sign, and the house where your Sun was located is the other half of that puzzle. For instance, if your Sun were in the sign of Libra in House 5—you would be a Libra/Leo. This is because the energy of House 5 is rooted in Leo (each house mimics the energy undertones of the signs). The first House represents the energy of Aries, the second Taurus, the third Gemini, the fourth Cancer, so forth and so on.

We are jumping ahead of ourselves though, because we must first learn the shortcut to interpreting the signs of the zodiac. As we learned in chapter one, the zodiac is broken up into 12 segments and 12 corresponding zodiac signs. Each of these signs is a representation of a specific type of energy and approach to life. From Aries to Pisces, these approaches to life are all a part of who each and every one of us are, but we each have a different distribution of these energies. Luckily, each of these 12 Signs relates to a group of archetypal patterns—from The Warrior to The Nurturer, these energy patterns can relate back to each of the zodiac signs. Thus, we can discover the energy of the sign through its corresponding archetype.

Viewing the zodiac through the lens of the archetypes is a very valuable tool and it allows us to impute various understandings we already have. In this chapter, we will learn which archetype represents each sign and how that expresses. When we approach the signs in this manner, you'll find that you can ascend above mere memorization and call upon a deeper knowing. All you will have to do is simply use the keys provided in the exercises, write down the active archetype for that sign, and listen to your internal response to the archetype. For instance, the archetype for Cancer is The Nurturer. Without knowing anything about the energy of the sign Cancer, based on the archetype of The Nurturer you can begin to form a frame of reference. In this case, you may automatically begin to form a construct around The Nurturer—someone kind, giving, and maternal.

The planets are the alphabet in astrology and how we interpret them is based on their location in your Natal Chart. Both the house location and zodiac sign that each of these planets are in helps to determine the approach to life we will take. Your Sun relates to the ego-driven nature of your personality. This tends to be a driving energy behind how you will choose to express your unique spiritual personality. The Sun will appear in your Natal Chart in its specific sign and in a specific house that is unique to you. This is why I said earlier that your sign, which correlates to the position of the Sun in the Tropical Zodiac, is only half of the story for its expression. I was born with my Sun in Taurus (The Builder) in the House of Gemini (The Storyteller). When it comes

to the ego-expression expressed by the position of the Sun, I have both the traits of a Taurus and a Gemini.

If we look at the two signs activated by the Sun through their corresponding archetypes, we begin to fit the puzzle pieces of your personality together. As I described above, your Sun is in a sign and in a house (that activates another sign!). Let's see how this small difference in active signs/ archetypes can have such a huge impact on the simple interpretation that many of us already know. Let's look at Gemini and its archetype, The Storyteller. We can already impute that The Storyteller would have communication as a large driving force in their life—they like telling stories! The placement in the houses will be activating another archetype and will shape the expression of the first. If the Sun was in Gemini (The Storyteller) in House 4 (Cancer: The Nurturer) this expression may use communication to connect with others (Storyteller/Nurturer). What if the Sun was in a different house? What if it was in House 11, Aquarius: The Inventor? Now we are looking at a new expression of this energy and approach to life—one that will most likely use their communication in a problem-solving manner because they are extremely curious!

Now you've discovered one of the missing pieces to Sun Sign Astrology (the sign activated by house location), but the truth is, there are even more missing pieces. This is because the Sun is only one of the six dominant planets that are working together to form your unique personality. The Ascendant, Sun, Moon, Mercury, Venus, and Mars are all working together to create this specific personality. On top of this, each of the planets will have two archetypes activated in your Natal Chart (through zodiac sign and house locations). Once again, don't worry. We will work through each of these planets and activated archetypes in this exercise (when you are done you will have a list of your dominant archetypes and personality summary). Before we move forward, however, let's take a look at each sign and the archetype that it can be viewed through. Please note, each sign also lists the house it is associated with (because this is a very powerful piece).

House, Sign, Archetype

HOUSE	SIGN	ARCHETYPE
1	Aries	The Warrior
2	Taurus	The Builder
3	Gemini	The Storyteller
4	Cancer	The Nurturer
5	Leo	The Performer
6	Virgo	The Craftsman
7	Libra	The Peacemaker
8	Scorpio	The Alchemist
9	Sagittarius	The Philosopher
10	Capricorn	The Entrepreneur
11	Aquarius	The Inventor
12	Pisces	The Artist

House 1: Aries (The Warrior)

This is a very physical energy. It is tapped into the fight or flight process of the human body. Often adrenaline seeking and in deep need to feel alive and with purpose. This is a strong physical energy, and movement and exercise will be very important to maintaining this energy. This is the energy of the leader and does not like to be challenged because it wants to lead the way. It is extremely goal oriented and needs to be moving towards something at all times. They want to go their own way and are willing to fight the good fight (assuming they agree with it).

House 2: Taurus (The Builder)

This is an extremely resourceful energy because this is a working energy. It is looking to make everything they do have the most powerful effect possible. They are willing to work hard if they know they are going to reap the rewards and be able to relax when it is all said and done. This energy wants to make its own decisions and does not believe in being forced. If you try to force them, even if they believe in what

you said, they would stand on principle and not do it. Take note if you have any friends or family with this energy. It is best not to tell them what to do! They are also deeply sensual and will require physical contact to nourish their mind, body, and spirit. There is a tendency to stay with things far to long due to their natural loyalty—it is a very powerful practice for those with a lot of Taurus energy in their chart, to reassess commitments to ensure they are still serving their highest good.

House 3: Gemini (The Storyteller)

This energy is constantly seeking new ideas to thrill and delight themselves. They feel they must share and process all of the wonderful information they are collecting—oftentimes jumping from subject to subject because they love that feeling of being alive and refreshed! They find it hard to stick to one subject as they love the "newness" of discovery. They are most certainly a "people person" energy and consequently great at story telling and sales. With the chameleon-like powers, they are able to relate and adapt; they most certainly fit in wherever they go. Sometimes however, they have worn so many masks that they lose sight of who they really are. This makes it imperative for them to have something stable and repetitive in their life—often a significant other that loves their great tenacity and charm.

House 4: Cancer (The Nurturer)

This is an emotionally driven energy that is always seeking to find purpose in caring and connecting with others. They view themselves through the lens of relationships and, therefore, take the actions of others as a way of determining who they are. They naturally want to give, care for, and be responsible for others. There is a very strong Emotional Intelligence with this energy, but they can just as easily project their own thoughts and feelings onto others and become confused. To protect themselves (just as they protects others), they will shell up and become rather non-responsive when agitated (they avoid and cut you off when fearful). These are the collectors of the zodiac and subsequently have a tendency towards hoarding. This can apply to both physical items and emotional memories—they have a hard time letting go because the energy defines itself through experiences with others.

House 5: Leo (The Performer)

This energy lives for the response of an audience and wants to perform in some manner through a creative expression. You will find that there is a childlike innocence and playful approach to life—one that is optimistic and ready to shine. This energy is infectious, and you will always be smiling when there is a Leo in the room. They simply entertain on so many levels! They will always be very generous and eager to please, unless of course you don't say thank you (they go for the reaction after all!). There is an undertone of royalty to this energy and they feel they deserve very much in this life (sometimes this can be misinterpreted). Where some manage, Leo leads.

House 6: Virgo (The Craftsman)

This energy is about making sense out of chaos and organizing along the way—always fine tuning a skill or a craft. This is a meticulous energy that is very analytical and prone to too much thought about everything. This is the right-hand man, always wanting to influence on a greater scale, but with no desire to have the final say or be in the spot light (too much anxiety around that). There is a great need to serve from this energy and to help others through practical application rather than emotional connection.

House 7: Libra (The Peacemaker)

This energy is all about relationships and seeing as many points of view as possible. Where Leo thrived on entertaining the audience, Libra needs the personal interaction of the one-on-one. This energy sees in shades of gray and does not understand black and white (decisions are complicated things that need to be contemplated). Often able to see and agree with all pros and cons, it makes it hard to commit to a decision, thus procrastination is inevitable! When feeling a little feisty, they love nothing more than a good debate. They like to debate for debate's sake and will easily take whatever side (they see both always!). This is a person-pleasing energy and one that is naturally very sociable and popular. Don't be misled, however; if you push them too far, they will eventually snap and bring things back into balance.

House 8: Scorpio (The Alchemist)

This is the sexiest, most charismatic energy in the whole zodiac: a charmer, a skeptic, and a mystic. The Alchemist is all about turning water into gold and ultimately—control, control, control. It is full of lust and passion with a very intense and inquisitive mind. This energy is the only sign in the zodiac represented by two animals—the scorpion and the eagle—which is why Scorpio is known for hitting the low lows and high heights. Being deeply intuitive, they have the uncanny ability to capture the attention of whomever they desire on multiple levels. They not only seek to connect, but they seek to control. This energy is at its best when it is using its charm for the greater good and using its passion to uncover vital knowledge for humanity. Also known for the ability to manage, attract, and raise large sums of money.

House 9: Sagittarius (The Philosopher)

This is the energy of the lifetime student and philosopher—always seeking more knowledge and never feeling like it can acquire enough! This lover of thought and pondering will desire great journeys and odysseys in their life. They are happy to teach and are always generous with knowledge. Made for greatness, this energy tends to avoid the mundane responsibilities of life. A boring job and house chores hold little allure to this active mind. This energy blossoms most when it sees the benefit of how their daily affairs impact the greater journey of their life (this will always be their struggle). If it weren't for earning money to fund their expeditions, they would most likely never sign up willingly for these day-to-day tasks.

House 10: Capricorn (The Entrepreneur)

This is an old and wise energy—older beyond its years. It is the energy of the natural commander, ready to make sense and order for the people. Because this energy has strong morals and ethics, they find it hard to act in any way that does not align with their strong character. This energy often works best for itself and is a natural entrepreneur (hard working, ever persevering energy that is in it for the long haul). This energy wants to work hard for work's sake. It loves to accomplish goals and wants to feel as if its life has meaning. Drawn to providing for its people, it will naturally seek leadership opportunities. People with this energy will protect without hesitation and fight for those they hold dear (even to their own detriment).

House 11: Aquarius (The Inventor)

This is a problem-solving energy that is constantly seeking new knowledge and answers! People with this energy innately want to challenge the status quo and bring society to the next level—through whatever means they can. This energy can push in several different directions and is often drawn to advancement through technology or humanitarian efforts. They have a level of emotional detachment (how can you not when you are constantly seeking problems and trying to fix them?). This emotional detachment is a way to accomplish more work in their life and affect more people. We know how the nurturing energy of Cancer could get weighed down, but Aquarius people do things differently—they truly are ready to advance the world.

House 12: Pisces (The Artist)

This is an artistic, empathetic energy seeking to always connect and create. It has the archetype of The Artist and The Dreamer. With its insatiable hunger to connect and help others, they often take on the energy patterns of those around them—easily becoming exhausted and plagued with the very ills they are trying to combat. Pisces has the strongest and most accurate intuition in the zodiac, but due to its very caring nature, it can easily become confused. Not knowing where their energy ends and another's begins proves to be the most difficult feat for them to overcome. The dreamer and keeper of all invisible, it explores the deeper questions of this life. Why are we here? What is our purpose? How can I help? It is the energy of many disciplines that have the objective of connection: The Healing Counselor, The Artist, The Actor/Actress, and The Musician. At its core, people with this energy want one thing: to connect and make an impact on the world through an artistic medium.

In this exercise, you will look at the archetypes/signs that are activated by these inner planets. By doing so, you end up with a very accurate interpretation of your personality because each planet represents a different facet of your very complex personality. For instance, the Ascendant represents how others experience you, while the Sun represents how your ego is trying to approach life. The Moon represents your instinctual/emotional self and Mercury represents your mind and communication style. Venus represents your approach to love and values and Mars how you choose to take action. Together,

they form all the pieces of the puzzle when it comes to your internal personality expression—your main tool for experiencing life.

Let's look at the astrological personality perspective of Abraham Lincoln based on his Natal Chart. Following is a breakdown of the five dominant inner planets and his Ascendant.

A snapshot of the archetypes activated within the Natal Chart of Abraham Lincoln:

PLANET	MEANING	ZODIAC	HOUSE	ACTIVATED
Ascendant/ Rising Sign	How the world experiences your energy	Aquarius	N/A	Inventor
Sun	Ego expression	Aquarius	House 1: Aries	Inventor / Warrior
Moon	Instinctual self	Capricorn	House 12: Pisces	Entrepreneur / Artist
Mercury	Mind & communications	Pisces	House 1: Aries	Artist / Warrior
Venus	Approach to love and values	Aries	House 2: Taurus	Warrior / Builder
Mars	How you take action	Libra	House 8: Scorpio	Peacemaker / Alchemist

In the table, we are able to see the 11 archetypes active within his personality. We are looking now for patterns and repeated archetypes that show up in his Natal Chart. His dominant archetypes are as follows:

The Warrior (3)
The Artist (2)
The Inventor (2)
The Entrepreneur (1)
The Peacemaker(1)
The Builder(1)
The Alchemist(1)

Once you have determined the dominant archetypes of a chart, it's useful to read back through the short description for each sign. Reading the descriptions of the two most dominant archetypes, The Warrior and The Artist, I would discover that The Warrior is the energy of the leader and someone willing to fight for what they believe in. In fact, they *need* that level of adrenaline pumping through their veins. Learning more about The Artist, I would discover that there is a deep need to connect and

have purpose and meaning in this life. Putting these two archetypes together, I can determine that Lincoln had the fight of The Warrior and the heart of The Artist seeking to help and heal.

Because Lincoln's second dominant archetype was actually a tie between The Artist and The Inventor, I know that they both pull equal weight. Reading about the Inventor, I would discover that this energy is always seeking to challenge the status quo and bring about social change. I can add on to the assessment earlier by saying he had the fight of The Warrior and the heart of The Artist seeking to help and heal by bringing about some new way of doing things (The Inventor).

We can't simply forget the other remaining archetypes however: The Entrepreneur, The Peacemaker, The Builder, and The Alchemist. These are still a part of the mix in Lincoln's personality, adding the additional energetic approach that he would take in this life. In order to create a personality summary, I will pull one word that resonates with each of these archetypes to finish painting the picture. He had the fight of The Warrior and the heart of The Artist seeking to heal and help by bringing about some new ways of doing things. Independent. Peace-seeking. Efficient. Change-inducing.

As you complete the exercise, you will discover the dominant archetypes of your personality. You will sift through this knowledge and create a short personality summary (just like we did for Abraham Lincoln). Challenge yourself in this exercise! Detach and view yourself as the archetypes you just learned about in your Natal Chart. If you have five or more of the same archetype, you can bet that you picked that for a unique reason before incarnating into this life. The more you have of an archetype, the more powerful it becomes (and oftentimes the more difficult to manage).

Once you get rolling with the power of the archetypes, you will be guided through which archetype rules over each of the houses in your chart. In the first chapter, we discovered that each house represents different areas of physical manifestation. It is the "where" that these energy dynamics will show up in our lives. For instance, House 9 is about travel, education, and writing; someone who has the archetype of The Entrepreneur in House 9 would travel for different reasons than say The Performer.

Remember, your time of birth is used as the "tuning fork" to draw the 12 signs of the zodiac into your chart. Aries, the first sign of the zodiac holds a special importance in your chart. This house will receive heightened importance in your development of self and you will feel a strong connection to the areas of life that this house rules. In the second exercise for this chapter, you will explore the influence of the signs in the houses and specifically the significance of Aries. For example, Aries rules House 3 in my chart, which means my identity and understanding of self is deeply connected to the areas ruled by that house (communication) and the energy of the sign associated with that house Gemini (The Storyteller). If you have a chart where Aries rules two houses, both houses will be of importance.

It's time for you to now see what the archetypes can reveal about your life experience: first by discovering the archetypes active within you and then by seeing how they stretch into the specific areas of life! Each sign is now represented by a specific archetype. Dig deep within yourself and begin to visualize how this energy acts and expresses itself. This will be one of the primary tools we continue to use throughout the entire spiritual workbook. As we explore various concepts we will continually build upon this foundation.

Start Your Exercises!
PERSONALITY ARCHETYPES

Your primary tool for experiencing your earthly incarnation is your personality—discover what archetypes triumph.

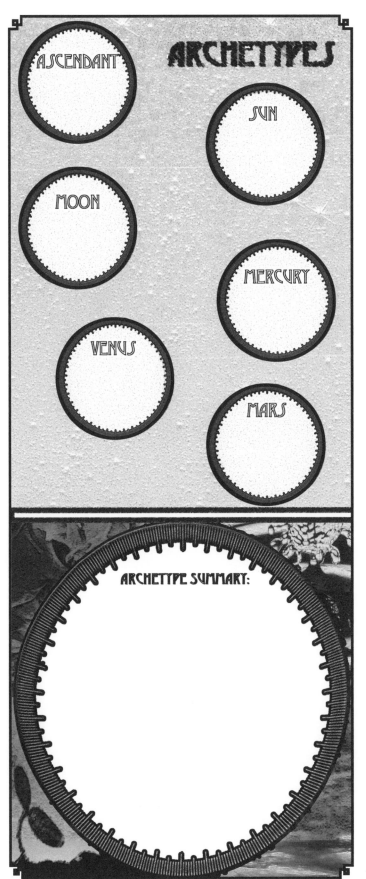

ARCHETYPES

ASCENDANT

SUN

MOON

MERCURY

VENUS

MARS

ARCHETYPE SUMMARY:

EXERCISE
Personality Archetypes

STEP 1:

In this exercise, you will identify the two archetypes activated by each inner planet in your Natal Chart.

1. In Table 1 of your Natal Chart Navigator, look up each sign and house location for the inner planets (listed in the circles on the left of the worksheet). The key below indicates the house number and active archetype for that house.

2. Once you determine the active archetypes, write them into the appropriate circles. For instance, if you have the Sun in Aries in House 2, you would enter Warrior/Builder in the Sun circle. Please note, the Ascendant only activates an archetype by zodiac sign and not by house. Therefore, you will only write one archetype in for that circle.

House 1	Aries	The Warrior
House 2	Taurus	The Builder
House 3	Gemini	The Storyteller
House 4	Cancer	The Nurturer
House 5	Leo	The Performer
House 6	Virgo	The Craftsman
House 7	Libra	The Peacemaker
House 8	Scorpio	The Alchemist
House 9	Sagittarius	The Philosopher
House 10	Capricorn	The Entrepreneur
House 11	Aquarius	The Inventor
House 12	Pisces	The Artist

STEP 2:

Add up each of the archetypes present and list them sequentially into the blank rectangle below. This will show you which archetypes are the most powerful forces within your spirit and current personality.

STEP 3:

1. Using the example from the chapter, create a sentence describing your unique archetype blend by using the top two to create a sentence.

2. Use the remaining archetypes to generate a one- or two-word summary and insert them after your sentence in the blank circle to the left. This is a powerful way that you can connect with your internal mission for this life and embrace who you are.

Everyone has 12 houses in their Natal Chart, but the energy ruling over each of these houses varies based on the signs that rule them. Look to Table 2 of your Natal Chart Navigator to determine each House Ruler and Secondary Ruler in your chart as you complete the steps below.

STEP 1:

For each of the 12 houses you will write in the specific archetypes activated by the ruling signs in your chart. Using the archetype key on the House Exploration and the Archetypes worksheet, look up each sign from Table 2 and then enter this information into the appropriate house.

* Please note, there are three blank segments for each house. Write the Ruling Archetype into the outermost blank segment and then the secondary rulers into the innermost ones.

STEP 2:

You can learn a lot from this exercise, but I want to draw your attention to a specific house. The house ruled by Aries (The Warrior), represents the area of your life that will play a significant role in your development of self. For instance, if you have the House Ruler of Aries (The Warrior) in House 10, career and leadership would be integral in your path to self-actualization. On the other hand, if you have Aries (The Warrior) in House 4, your sense of self would develop primarily through your family and early home environment.

Once you find the house that is ruled by The Warrior (Aries), write that information into the inner circle.

The signs leave an energetic impression unique to you in each of the 12 Astrological Houses. Discover how they are creating their dynamic pull.

HOUSE EXPLORATION AND THE ARCHETYPES

ARCHETYPE KEY

ARIES: THE WARRIOR

TAURUS: THE BUILDER

GEMINI: THE STORYTELLER

CANCER: THE NURTURER

LEO: THE PERFORMER

VIRGO: THE CRAFTSMAN

LIBRA: THE PEACEMAKER

SCORPIO: THE ALCHEMIST

SAGITTARIUS: THE PHILOSOPHER

CAPRICORN: THE ENTREPRENEUR

AQUARIUS: THE INVENTOR

PISCES: THE ARTIST

*The planets are God's
punctuation marks pointing
the sentences of human fate,
written in the constellations.*

—James Lendall Basford (1845–1915),
Seven Seventy Seven Sensations, 1897

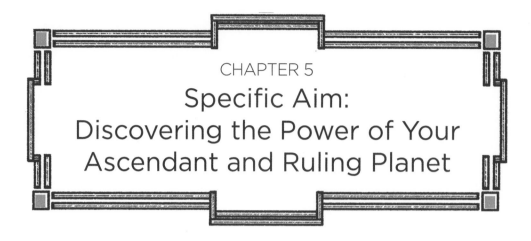

CHAPTER 5

Specific Aim: Discovering the Power of Your Ascendant and Ruling Planet

POWER PLAN

○ Discover your personal power phrase through your Ascendant
○ Learn what planets rule your chart and provide more insight into your life purpose
○ Determine your current life's aim by applying these concepts to your chart

Now that you have begun to experience the power and accuracy of Astrology, wouldn't it be nice to get a little more specific? We already discovered the general direction of your life by determining your True North through the Moon Nodes. Now it is time to focus in even more and determine your specific life aim. We do this by assessing your Ascendant and Ruling Planet. Each step we take will uncover a piece of this puzzle and by the end of this chapter, you will have assembled each of these individual pieces to determine your specific life aim.

Each individual has a unique life aim, but all of these aims begin with one of the 12 personal power phrases below. As we complete your specific life aim, we will also take a deeper look at the aim of Steve Jobs. His Ascendant is at 22°Virgo and the phrase for Virgo is, "I Analyze." We can deduce that part of Steve Jobs' specific aim in his life was "To Analyze."

This is a powerful process where we will begin to reveal some of the deeper energetic work that you came into this life to achieve. At the moment of your birth, the stars were in perfect harmony with your being. They were an exact reflection of the spiritual state of your consciousness and literally reflect back the specific energy that you brought into this life. Just as you would look to a physical mirror to view the reflection of your physical body, we look to the natal birth chart to reflect the spiritual body.

The Natal Chart is specifically reflecting information about your life, your consciousness, and your intentions for this life. The beauty of the exercise we are going to be working on in this chapter is that you will begin to see your life through a new lens. This may or may not be a difficult process for you, but either way I guarantee that you will be able to shift yourself energetically into a new more expansive space—where you see your life as a continuum of patterns that are seeking to evolve and reveal themselves to you.

You may have heard astrologers mention ruling planets or chart rulers. This is often snuck into interpretation or commentary, but can be a little bit hard to understand if you are not familiar with astrology. Your chart ruler is indeed a very important piece of the picture because it is reflecting specific information about your nature and your life aim. The chart ruler is allowing you the opportunity to investigate the pathway in which you will undergo the most amount of growth in your life.

As we continue on, keep in mind that your chart ruler is determined by the sign of your Ascendant/ Rising Sign. All of the 12 Signs have a planet that rules them. There is a deep connection between the planets and the signs in astrology. It is often the deeper layer to interpreting the information in the chart and offers the additional insights that help us unlock the hidden messages in your chart.

As we dive in deeper throughout this chapter, take your time and focus on releasing and stepping outside of yourself. This chapter is about taking basic pieces of a puzzle and putting them together in a way that is unique to you and being birthed through your awareness. As we take each piece of the puzzle, we will be placing them together in a way that allows you to create a coherent sentence that will serve as validation to your path. I often see a sparkle emerge in the eyes of my clients when they begin to see how this life aim is deeply connected to the inner pull they have felt their entire life.

As you read the chapter, focus on simply absorbing the information. The exercise will guide you through this process step by step; you don't need to worry about piecing all of your information together right away (even though you probably will want to). This chapter will be focusing specifically on the importance of your Ascendant (Rising Sign) and the planets associated with that sign through rulership. Remember, each sign has a planet ruler because they are deeply connected. Astrology is a beautiful language that pieces together energy patterns that translate into deep insights in the physical world.

The phrase "To Analyze" isn't random. Each of the 12 zodiac signs has a saying that relates to the energy pattern that is most dominant within that sign. For instance, Virgo is "I Analyze," but Pisces is "I Believe." Virgo is known for its attention to detail and its meticulous need to make sense out of chaos (The Craftsman)—hence the phrase, "I

Analyze." Pisces on the other hand is the energy of the dreamer and its archetype is The Artist. This energy is seeking to know the invisible—hence its phrase "I Believe." Each of the 12 signs has their specific distinguishing phrase and the sign of your Ascendant holds the key to your very own personal power phrase.

Using the chart that follows, locate the sign of your Ascendant (see Table 1 columns 1 and 2 under Sensitive Points of your Natal Chart Navigator) and its unique phrase (go ahead and circle it).

Personal Power Phrases

SIGN	PERSONAL POWER PHRASE
Aries	I Am
Taurus	I Have
Gemini	I Think
Cancer	I Feel
Leo	I Will
Virgo	I Analyze
Libra	I Balance
Scorpio	I Desire
Sagittarius	I Aim
Capricorn	I Utilize
Aquarius	I Know
Pisces	I Believe

With this first step completed, we will now move towards figuring out the rest of the puzzle. We know that Steve Jobs is here "To Analyze" based on the sign of his Ascendant. But how can we know to what aim or purpose? To discover the next portion of your specific aim, we look to the Ruling Planet of your chart.

Each sign in the zodiac has a Ruling Planet and this is where the planet is said to be in "rulership" because the planet is working in harmony with the sign. The Ruling Planet of your chart is subsequently the Ruling Planet of your Ascendant. If you have Taurus as your Ascendant, you have Venus as the Ruling Planet of your chart because Venus rules Taurus. If you have Scorpio as your Ascendant, you have Pluto as your Ruling Planet because Pluto rules Scorpio. Once again, don't worry about memorizing anything. This chapter and the exercise will provide you with all the information you need to determine your specific life aim.

Each zodiac sign is 30 degrees, and the first 10 degrees of each sign has only one Ruling Planet. This means that if your Ascendant is located within the first 10° of the zodiac sign that it occupies, it will activate only one Ruling Planet. However (and here is where it gets slightly more complicated), if your Ascendant is either between 10°-19° or 20°-29° it will also activate another planet as well. But let's take it one step at a time…

Once you determine the planet that rules your Ascendant, you will look to the specific sign and house where it is located in your chart. For Steve Jobs, Virgo's Ruling Planet is Mercury. Mercury for him is located in the sign Aquarius (The Inventor) and in House 5 (the House of Performing and Creative Expression). With this information, I am able to say that his specific aim in this life is roughly, To Analyze (Virgo Ascendant) through invention (Mercury in Aquarius) in some sort of creative expression or performance (Mercury in the 5th). Because he has his Ascendant at 22°Virgo though, I know that there is more going on with his specific aim (he has more than one planet ruling his chart).

Each of the signs has thirty degrees, and the first ten degrees of that sign picks up the specific energy of that element. For instance, if you have 9°Taurus, you would be picking up just on the Taurus energy. However, all of the 30° of each sign carries within it the DNA of the entire element it represents. If you remember from the first chapter, each sign is made up of an element and mode. There are four Elements: Fire, Earth, Air, and Water and this pattern repeats itself three times to complete the 12 signs of the zodiac. Within each 30° of each sign, there is a representation of all three of the signs with the same element (each getting 10°).

Let's look at Taurus: the first 10° of the sign belongs to the originator (Taurus). However, when we reach 10°–19° it also carries the energy of the next Earth sign (Virgo). If the Ascendant then is 15°Taurus, we are picking up on Taurus and Virgo—thus the Ruling Planet of each (Venus and Mercury). If the Ascendant is 25°Taurus, it would be activating the second Earth sign following it, Capricorn. We still have Venus as a Ruling Planet, but now we also add the planet that rules Capricorn, Saturn. This is how each of the signs works throughout the zodiac—each 30 degrees holds the energy patterns for the signs with that same element. This concept is particularly important when assessing the life aim due to the influence of the Ruling Planets (this is the only instance we will use this specific information and these are referred to as deacons).

Don't worry if it is too complicated to follow! All you really need to do is look at the chart that follows and find your Ascendant sign—once located, look at the column that correlates with the degree of your Ascendant and jot down your Ruling Planets in the exercise.

Ruling Planets based on the degree and sign of your Ascendant/Rising Sign:

SIGN	0°	10°-20°	20°-30°
Aries	Mars	Mars and Sun	Mars and Jupiter
Taurus	Venus	Venus and Mercury	Venus and Saturn
Gemini	Mercury	Mercury and Venus	Mercury and Uranus
Cancer	Moon	Moon and Pluto	Moon and Neptune
Leo	Sun	Sun and Jupiter	Sun and Mars
Virgo	Mercury	Mercury and Saturn	Mercury and Venus
Libra	Venus	Venus and Uranus	Venus and Mercury
Scorpio	Pluto	Pluto and Neptune	Pluto and Moon
Sagittarius	Jupiter	Jupiter and Mars	Jupiter and Sun
Capricorn	Saturn	Saturn and Venus	Saturn and Mercury
Aquarius	Uranus	Uranus and Mercury	Uranus and Venus
Pisces	Neptune	Neptune and Moon	Neptune and Pluto

Remember, the Ruling Planet always holds its influence regardless of whether you have a second Ruling Planet in your chart. If your Ascendant is in Virgo, no matter what degree, Mercury will always be your Ruler. The additional Ruling Planets are co-rulers so to speak. Let's take a look again at Steve Jobs Ascendant at 22°Virgo. He has the Ruling Planets: Mercury and Venus. Now is the fun part! We get to determine his specific life aim.

We already interpreted that he was here to analyze as The Inventor in some creative art or performing capacity. Now we are going to add the Venus (second Ruling Planet) piece to see what his specific aim was in his life. In his chart, Venus is located in Capricorn (The Entrepreneur) in House 4 (Private, Personal, and Family). Let's see what we come up with: To analyze (Virgo Ascendant) as The Inventor (Mercury in Aquarius) to create (Mercury in the 5th) as an entrepreneur (Venus in Capricorn) something for the private, personal, and family (Venus in the 4th). Let's make that a little more eloquent! In this life, Steve Jobs was here to analyze and create by being an Inventor and would be an Entrepreneur bringing something new to the personal, family, and home. I would have to say that his inventions are extremely creative and certainly do impact the personal, family, and home!

Shall we do one more before you do your own? Let's revisit Mother Teresa since we have already looked at her Moon Nodes. Her Ascendant is at 22°Sagittarius so we know she was activating the, "I Aim." At 22° we know she has two Ruling Planets: Jupiter and the Sun. She has Jupiter in Libra (The Peacemaker) in House 9 (Travel, Education, Philosophy). She has the Sun in Virgo (The Craftsman) in House 9 as well. If I were to put this together, I could say she was aiming to be a Peacemaker through travel, education, and philosophy using her craft.

Each specific life aim is unique and must draw on the placement of the Ruling Planets. By adding this information to the direction of your life through the Moon Nodes, you are now able to gain much insight into your life purpose. I know that it can be a very intimidating thing—to know that you are here with a purpose, and there is a specific life aim that you are meant to realize. My suspicion is that many of us know these things deep down inside, but we are ambivalent in recognizing our own potential. Discovering our purpose is how we begin to move forward and learn to trust our gifts and ourselves. Accept this insight into your life and know that it serves as deep validation; your life has a specific purpose. You are now beginning to see how you can claim your power—by first beginning to understand why you are here.

Start Your Exercise!
PERSONAL LIFE AIM

Get your creative juices flowing as you piece together the puzzle of your personal life aim.

See sample worksheet on pages 114–115

EXERCISE
Personal Life Aim

In this exercise you will determine your personal life aim through the power of your Ascendant. You will need to utilize the chart in the chapter to determine the planets that rule your chart. There will either be one or two planets based on the degree of your Ascendant. Follow the steps that follow to piece together this information.

STEP 1:

1. The first thing you will need to do to determine your life aim is to discover your personal power phrase. (You may have already circled your phrase on the worksheet!) Based on the sign of your Ascendant (see Table 1 columns 1 and 2 under Sensitive Points on your Natal Chart Navigator), look to the key to the right to determine the first portion of your personal aim.

2. Once you determine your power phrase, write it into the triangle on the Personal Life Aim worksheet at the top.

STEP 2:

1. Now you will need to utilize the chart on page 42 to determine which planets rule your chart (based on the degree of your Ascendant). Remember, if the degree is between 10–30, then you will have two planets ruling your chart.

2. Enter the planet or planets into the circles just below your personal aim.

STEP 3:

1. Now that you have determined the planets ruling your chart, it is time to find out what they mean. Based on the location of the Ruling Planet, use the zodiac sign in which it is located to determine the archetype that is helping you to fulfill your life aim. You can find this information in Table 1, Columns 1 and 2.

2. Write the archetype in the circle connected to the Ruling Planet on the worksheet. If you have two Ruling Planets, make sure to write in the archetype of the other planet as well.

STEP 4:

1. To determine the area of life that the life aim is taking place in, we need to determine the house location of the Ruling Planets in your Natal Chart. Once you determine the house location use the key to determine the area of life activated. You can find this information in Table 1, Columns 1 and 4.

2. Enter the area into the circle connected to the archetype. If you have two Ruling Planets, make sure to do this for both of the planets.

STEP 5:

Now it is time to finish your life aim sentence by choosing the words needed to complete it. This is an opportunity for you to draw on all of your life experiences so far to put your life aim together. Take a moment to think about all the things that have happened in your life. The events, people, and places you have experienced. Think about who you are as a personality and why you may have chosen to incarnate with these specific traits. When you're ready, complete your life aim sentence. One you complete the fill in the blank life aim directions, enter them into the rectangle under "Your Life Aim."

Personal Power Phrase

Aries: I am
Taurus: I have
Gemini: I think
Cancer: I feel
Leo: I will
Virgo: I analyze
Libra: I balance
Scorpio: I desire
Sagittarius: I aim
Capricorn: I utilize
Aquarius: I know
Pisces: I believe

Sign Archetypes

Aries: The Warrior
Taurus: The Builder
Gemini: The Storyteller
Cancer: The Nurturer
Leo: The Performer
Virgo: The Craftsman
Libra: The Peacemaker
Scorpio: The Alchemist
Sagittarius: The Philosopher
Capricorn: The Entrepreneur
Aquarius: The Inventor
Pisces: The Artist

House Areas

1: Self-development
2: Attaining Resources
3: Communication
4: Family Connection
5: Creative/Playful
6: Service/Efficiency
7: Partnership
8: Spiritual Rebirth
9: Written Word/Philosophy
10: Career/Leadership
11: Humanitarian
12: Spiritual Belief/Art

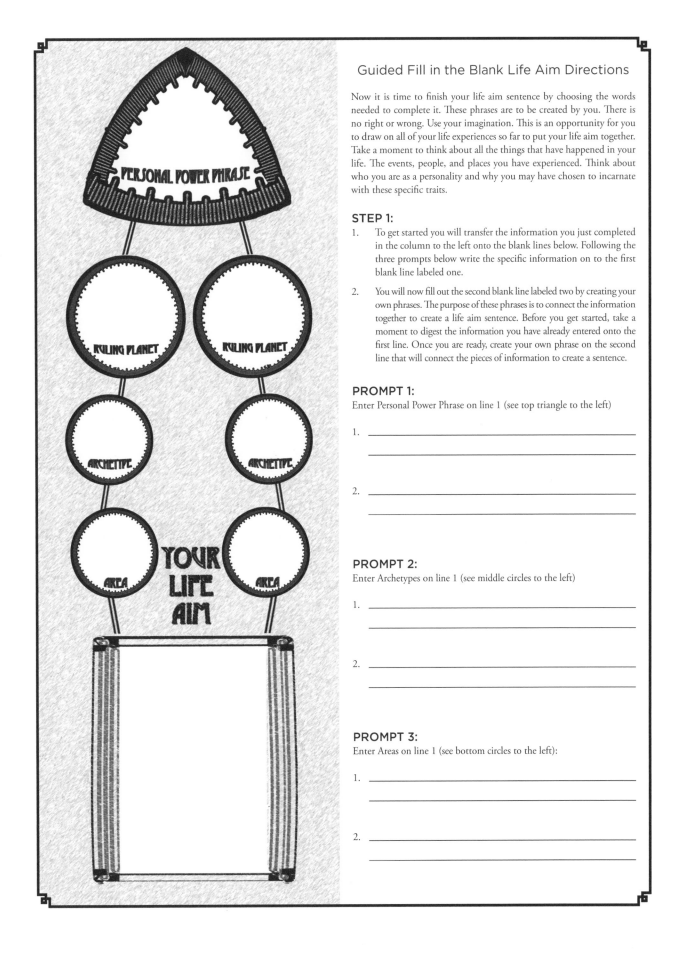

Guided Fill in the Blank Life Aim Directions

Now it is time to finish your life aim sentence by choosing the words needed to complete it. These phrases are to be created by you. There is no right or wrong. Use your imagination. This is an opportunity for you to draw on all of your life experiences so far to put your life aim together. Take a moment to think about all the things that have happened in your life. The events, people, and places you have experienced. Think about who you are as a personality and why you may have chosen to incarnate with these specific traits.

STEP 1:

1. To get started you will transfer the information you just completed in the column to the left onto the blank lines below. Following the three prompts below write the specific information on to the first blank line labeled one.

2. You will now fill out the second blank line labeled two by creating your own phrases. The purpose of these phrases is to connect the information together to create a life aim sentence. Before you get started, take a moment to digest the information you have already entered onto the first line. Once you are ready, create your own phrase on the second line that will connect the pieces of information to create a sentence.

PROMPT 1:
Enter Personal Power Phrase on line 1 (see top triangle to the left)

1. _____
_____

2. _____
_____

PROMPT 2:
Enter Archetypes on line 1 (see middle circles to the left)

1. _____
_____

2. _____
_____

PROMPT 3:
Enter Areas on line 1 (see bottom circles to the left):

1. _____
_____

2. _____
_____

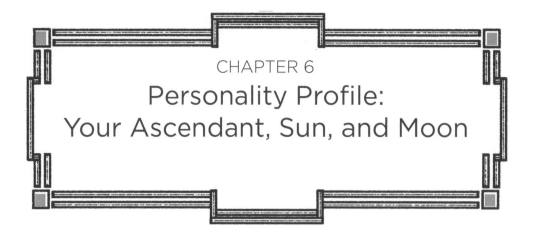

CHAPTER 6
Personality Profile:
Your Ascendant, Sun, and Moon

POWER PLAN

△ Explore how others perceive your energy personality
△ Determine your Astrological Name through the Ascendant, Sun, and Moon
△ Use the signs to gain awareness as to how others experience your personality

One of the first things we do when we meet someone new is discover their name. Who they are becomes intertwined with their name in our subconscious—it is a shortcut our mind uses for storing the information we learn about them. This first impression we have will always stick with us. Sometimes we go beyond this and interact with the larger part of their being, but in most cases we continue to interact with this snippet of who they are. And just as we do this for each and every person we meet, they each do the same thing back to us. They are seeing a snippet version of who we are and this is our personality profile. It is the Cliffs Notes of the complexity within our charts (within ourselves). It is who people come to know as "you" that aren't intricately woven into your inner life.

What we determine in these brief encounters with other spirits changes how we act towards them. As we assess and interact with them, we will continue to look at them through this initial lens and personality profile. We do this because it helps tell us a lot about who they are in a short amount of time. It is a way that we have learned to filter who we let in to our lives and who we

hold back. Without realizing it, this personality profile that we experience of others (and others experience of us) can be expressed in one of two ways: the higher expression or the lower expression. Each sign has a root function, but there is always choice in how that energy is expressed, and sometimes this can work against us.

Let's face it, trying to understand how others perceive us is a very difficult thing to do (good thing we have astrology!). No one in a short amount of time can begin to grasp who you are entirely, and you can't separate from your complexity. The best others can do (really the only thing they can do) is to pick up on this personality profile: Your Rising Sign, Sun, and Moon. Beginning to understand how people experience us in this life is one very powerful way in which we can claim our personal power. Then we can ask the difficult questions: Are we being perceived as we would like to be seen? Is it helping us to achieve our life aim?

Once we became aware of the initial impression we make, we can do a lot to control how we are perceived, but we must once again step away from ourselves. We must use astrology to help us gain a deeper awareness of how the rest of the world perceives us. This energetic personality profile is also your astrological name. It consists of the three most powerful energies in your chart: Your Rising Sign (Ascendant), Sun, and Moon. These three things are the Cliffs Notes to your chart, and for better or for worse, they are how others initially experience your energy.

I will always be "Capricorn Rising, Taurus Sun, Taurus Moon"—an instantaneously stubborn, hard-working, and ambitious energy (all earth signs and double Taurus to boot). When viewing them as the archetypes, I am The Entrepreneur, The Builder, The Builder. Because of this strong, almost forceful energy I have (three Earth and two in the same sign), it is of the utmost importance for me to soften myself when meeting others. As crazy as it sounds, the more I avoid declarative sentences and sharing my specific opinion on something, the better! There is very little I can do to change this personality profile, but what I can do is angle it for the best possible outcome.

We may never be able to change how we are perceived completely, but with a little bit of practice, we can begin to angle it in the most positive way possible. It was more than eye opening for me to discover this secret about myself. The "me" that people first meet—the "me" that is interacting with different people occasionally at work and in life. This simplified-cliff-notes-version of myself is something I never could have understood without astrology. Luckily, those we spend significant amounts of time with will know us beyond this personality profile (thank goodness!). But there will be very important people who come and go from your life that interact only with this snippet of who you are. It is for those people and those fate-determining moments that I feel this chapter is one of the most important in this book.

In this exercise, you will be looking at the zodiac sign of your Ascendant, Sun, and Moon. We have already explored each sign through the archetypes and now we will add the most common adjectives to describe each sign. Through the adjectives that describe each of the zodiac signs, you will be able to paint the picture of the personality profile that others experience of you. The Ascendant will be the most dominant, followed by the Sun, and then the Moon.

For instance, Marilyn Monroe's astrological name is Leo Rising, Gemini Sun, Aquarius Moon. I would first look at the adjectives to describe her Leo Rising (The Performer): playful, proud, loving, creative, performer, outgoing, generous, warm-hearted, bossy, patronizing, broad-minded, and enthusiastic. These adjectives reveal to us the most dominant interpretation of Marilyn Monroe's energy upon meeting her. Depending on the specific actions or things that she would have said, we would have been able to tune into the lower or higher vibrations of that particular energy. The adjectives to describe her Gemini Sun (The Storyteller) are: social, talkative, curious, outgoing, adaptable, versatile, inconsistent, nervous, intellectual, eloquent, loves to learn, and youthful. We would apply these adjectives to the dominant power of her Ascendant. Her Moon in Aquarius (The Inventor): innovative, humanitarian, ambitious, freedom seeker, humorous, challenges the status quo, detached, and problem solver. Together, these adjectives are showing us how she is first experienced upon meeting her, and she certainly was all of these things, but yet vastly more complex at the same time.

The energy surrounding others that you experience when you interact with them is the energy of the Ascendant, Sun, and Moon. Never forget that the same thing is happening to you when you are interacting with those who don't experience your full complexity. As you complete the exercise, take a moment to take it all in. How can you angle this energy for the most positive outcome? Are you aware of your energetic impact? How can you use this insight to achieve your life aim?

Start Your Exercise!
PERSONAL PROFILE

Step outside yourself to learn how others perceive you—
gain valuable clarity to enhance your first impression.

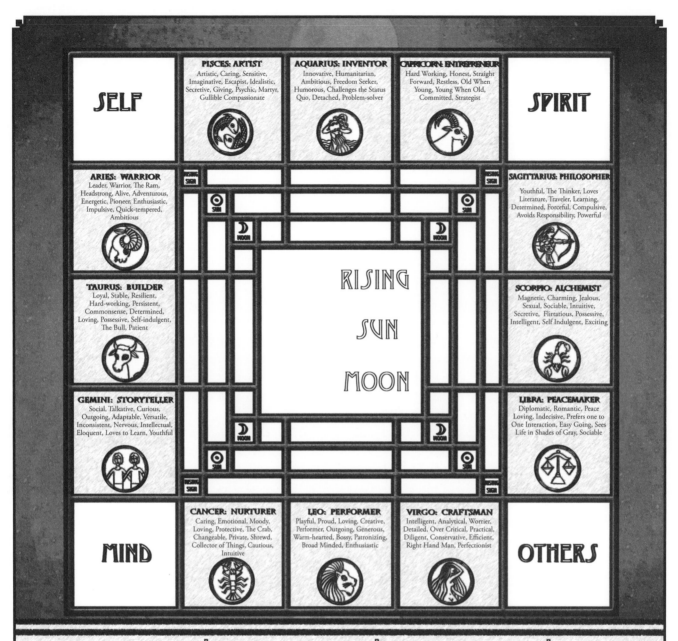

EXERCISE
Personal Profile

In this exercise we will be exploring the energies that make up your Astrological Name. These three powerful forces represent the spiritual recipe that offers you insight into how individuals outside your inner circle are experiencing your personality. Each of the outer squares represents a zodiac sign and the adjectives that describe how that energy can be interpreted. Each of the blank inner boxes correspond with the Rising Sign, Sun sign, and Moon sign (look in the corner squares to identify which one). Follow the steps that follow to reveal what it is that others are seeing.

STEP 1:

1. Enter your Astrological Name into the inner square above by filling in the blanks, i.e., Taurus Rising, Pisces Sun, Libra Moon by using the Natal Chart Navigator columns 1 and 2.

2. Now that you have identified the zodiac sign for your Rising Sign, Sun, and Moon look to the inner blank boxes. Shade the box for the zodiac sign activated. For example, the three boxes to the right of the square labeled Taurus are associated with Taurus.

STEP 2:

1. Each of these signs has words and adjectives to describe how these energies can be expressed. Remember, we are exploring these power players to gain insight into the cliff notes version of yourself. Read through all of the adjectives. Select three from each sign that you feel are the most accurate and write them in the space at the bottom right of your worksheet.

2. Now begin to meditate on the impact this has on those you meet.

STEP 3:

CHAPTER 7

The Main Players: Inner Planets, Social Planets, and Outer Planets

POWER PLAN

△ Understand the internal and external forces that affect your life journey
△ Learn about Inner, Social, and Outer Planets and their role in Natal Astrology
△ Discover what each outer planet can tell you about your life

Deciding to incarnate onto Earth is just like enrolling in school: we know that it may be challenging, but the rewards of the knowledge gained and the opportunities that will become available drive us to commit to seeing it through. Just as you would put the energy into choosing what college you would attend and the subject area you would want to study, we put that same level of thought into our current lives. This process acts as an accelerated learning program for our spiritual growth, and believe it or not, we jump into our lives eagerly to attain new heights of understanding.

Astrology can assist each of us in gaining insight and validation into the very purpose that inspired us to incarnate in the first place. As we experience life, we experience it on two distinct levels: internally and externally. This is largely how we are able to plan our lives and provide the opportunities to attain the life goals we set forth for ourselves while we are here. There is the internal level of our experience—that which houses our personality, thoughts, and emotions. Then there is the external level of our

experience—the events, circumstances, and people we interact with in the physical world.

This is a very important part of understanding how we chart our lives—we choose things that affect the internal and things that affect the external. For instance, prior to incarnating we are able to determine the type of personality we would like to have, the level of our intellect, the level of our intuition, and much more. By shaping these aspects of our internal level of life experience, we are paving a path that is uniquely created to help us achieve our goals. If you wanted a life in the spotlight, you would have inevitably picked a personality that was extroverted and pioneering. Those decisions are always made to help you achieve what you set out to do.

Conversely, we are very specific about the external environment we choose because we know the impact that it will have on the internal portion of our journey. We choose our parents specifically to help shape and mold our childhood in a way that was congruent with our life goal. We also picked many events and "check points" along the way, which continually provide us with opportunities to realize our goals. For instance, if you wanted to be fiercely independent—you would have chosen circumstances in your early childhood to help develop that trait. This is the external level happening "outside" us.

It is the interaction between the internal and external portions of our life journey here on Earth that creates such a marvelous platform for spiritual growth. The Natal Chart is your life's itinerary and it is capable of providing you with insight into what your plans were for this life. The planets can be separated into three distinct groups: The Inner Planets (Sun, Moon, Mercury, Venus, and Mars) the Social Planets (Jupiter and Saturn), and the Outer Planets (Uranus, Neptune, and Pluto). The inner planets are looking at what is happening inside of us and correspond to the internal experience of our life journey: The Sun provides insight into our ego, the Moon insight into our instinctual self/subconscious, Mercury how we learn and communicate, Venus how we love, and Mars how we choose to express our internal experience into actions in our external world. In chapter 4, you discovered the choices you made regarding the internal portion of your life experience by discovering your dominant archetypes.

The social planets (Jupiter and Saturn) and the outer planets (Uranus, Neptune, and Pluto) are giving us specific information about the external environment that we will be interacting with during our chosen incarnation. Jupiter and Saturn are extremely special planets in astrology and are described as both outer and social planets. While they are absolutely affecting our external environment, their main objective is to initiate the internal journey. This chapter is all about exploring these outer planets. This exploration can help answer some of the questions we've carried with us since childhood—"Why would I choose to be different?" "Why would I want to experience such difficulty in this area of my life?" "Why did this specific event occur?"

It is imperative to note (as always) that the direction of your Moon Nodes will oftentimes be a deciding factor in how you will interpret the information you gather from your chart. Take for instance an event, such as a relationship that you were highly invested in, coming to an end. Someone whose Moon Nodes indicate that they are moving from the "We" to the "I" (Quadrant 3 to 1) will react differently to a failed relationship than someone who is moving from "I" to "We" (Quadrant 3 to 1). The ending of a significant relationship for someone trying to gain independence in their current life (from "We" to "I") might act as a catalyst for them to move, change careers, or reinvent themselves. On the other hand, for someone who came here to learn about being in relationships (From "I" to "We"), it might cause them to become internally focused and head to a meditation retreat instead. The Moon Nodes are always available for you to dig deeper and to determine the likely outcome or purpose of a specific event that occurs in your life.

Let's look at the life of Michael Jackson as we begin to explore how these outer planets can impact our lives. The personality profile (Ascendant, Sun, Moon) for Michael Jackson is Pisces Rising, Pisces Moon, and Virgo Sun. Through the lens of the archetypes, we know that this translates to The Artist (Pisces), The Artist (Pisces), and the Craftsman (Virgo). Pisces is a Water sign and shows a highly sensitive spirit. As you will soon discover, when strong Pisces energy has taken on too much, it can often turn to drug addiction and escapism to cope with its stress. This is because Pisces energy is very sensitive to the energy of those around it—absorbing it all like a sponge: both the good and the bad. Unfortunately, Pisces has the potential to be so sympathetic and empathetic that it oftentimes is drawn more to sorrows of this world (fulfilling its deeper desire to serve). Michael Jackson had double Pisces in this power player trio (Ascendant, Sun, Moon), so we know Pisces was strong with him.

He had a Power Cluster of 5 planets in House 6 (Service, Work, and Physical Health). The Power Cluster consisted of three inner planets: Sun, Mercury, and Venus as well as two outer planets: Uranus and Pluto. Based on what we know about the archetypes, we know that his Sun was in Virgo in the House of Virgo, giving him a double archetype of The Craftsman. Virgo is always about organizing and seeking to perfect all that it does. It is a very self-critical energy that pushes itself to be its best, but sometimes does this to its own detriment. Venus and Mercury were also located in house 6 in the sign of Leo, The Performer. Remember, when there is an excessive amount of one particular archetype, it can be particularly hard to manage.

Putting this all together, we might say that this was a highly artistic energy (Pisces Rising, Pisces Moon), seeking the attention of others through performing (Leo Mercury, Leo Venus). There was a deep need to maintain perfection and to make sense of everything that occurred (House of Virgo with 5 planets). Due to the emphasized expression of Pisces and Virgo, he gained the artistic gifts, but the cost was the mental and emotional anguish that accompanied his heightened expression.

We have started building our understanding of Michael Jackson's chart through the placement of these inner planets, but we are missing one key piece. The direction of his Moon Nodes will specify what he was spiritually here to learn about in his life. In his life, Michael was moving from Quadrant 1 (South Node in House 2) to Quadrant 3 (North Node in House 8). This means he had many past lives where he was independent and self-reliant (Quadrant 1). In this life he was moving from the "I" into the "We" and beginning to explore his energy dynamic with others (Quadrant 3). His purpose was to grow and learn through his relationships, and this was a new experience for him.

Before we begin to look at the position of his outer planets, let's take a look at what each one of the outer planets signifies in Astrology.

JUPITER

This planet is known for its expansive and positive impact. It is the ruler of your spiritual development on the Earth plane and it supports you in the most positive way possible. The house that this planet occupies in your Natal Chart shows where you may have received early divine blessings. Because Jupiter is a Social Planet, it can also impact innate talents that you may have been born with. If you were a car, the Social Planets Jupiter and

Saturn relate to the traffic signs or speed limits you utilize while driving on the road. For instance, imagine you were driving to a very important event and you were stuck in traffic. Jupiter is when you hit that straight stretch of road with no traffic, and the speed limit goes up. This is where you can sit back, relax, and possibly make up for lost time.

SATURN

This planet is known for its constrictive and limiting impact. Through its rules and limitations we are pushed to achieve the most. Just like the teacher or coach who challenged you and helped you achieve all that you could, Saturn is this tough teacher. The location of Saturn in your chart will show you where the majority of your life lessons are to be learned. Saturn is like the traffic signals and stop signs—this makes driving a car a far more organized process. Saturn is telling you when to stop, yield, and go. The question you need to ask yourself is: Are you listening?

URANUS

This planet rules all things unusual in addition to unexpected change. Its location in your chart by house indicates the area of life where you would experience the "unusual." It can correlate with an area of life where you are exploring energy patterns that are not considered the "norm" according to society as a whole. This energy is often erratic and unpredictable.

NEPTUNE

This planet tends to be the most complicated of the outer planets. Its heart is rooted in unconditional love and total acceptance, but because it views life through this lens, it is often a dissolving influence in your life. It may be where you don't see things as they truly are and are easily misled. It is the "blind spot" of your life. One of the first things you're taught when learning to drive a car is that there is a blind spot. If you're not paying attention and you go to switch lanes without checking, there is the potential that you could misjudge the situation (you might miss the car in the rearview mirror and potentially go to switch lanes and cause a collision). We are taught to always double check and to physically turn our head and look, to check on the blind spot. The same thing applies to the blind spot caused by the placement of Neptune in the houses. This is the area of life where you will benefit greatly from seeking a second opinion and choosing to shy away from reacting too quickly.

PLUTO

This is the toughest of the outer planets. Where Saturn can act as the motivational teacher or coach, Pluto has the same goal: to help you achieve all that you can. The only difference is that it is a merciless energy that will force you to move forward. If you were meant to move to a new city and continuously denied yourself that intuitive pull, Pluto is the energy that would have your house destroyed in a storm so it could get you moving. It is the CEO of your spiritual growth, and it is concerned with your bottom line (growth in this life). Its placement in your chart represents the area for the most amount of spiritual growth, progress, and personal power.

In the next exercise, you will determine where the outer planets are located in your chart. Take a moment to consider the implications of each of these planets. It may be able to shed some light on a few things in your life that you've felt you didn't fully understand. For instance, if you discover that you have Uranus in House 8, it may provide

insight into your sexuality. Uranus is where you may express energy differently than what society considers its "norm" (the Scorpio energy of House 8 rules sexuality). By discovering the location of Uranus, you can see that this was the specific area you chose to be different in during this life. You can know without a shadow of a doubt, you wanted to experience that new expression of energy, regardless of how others viewed you.

As we explore the placement of these outer planets, we will come to see that it is the house location that is most important. This is because the outer planets have a lengthy orbit and stay in one sign for a significant amount of time. Their influence is felt in the individual based specifically on the location they take in the houses. Each of those houses have a core natural zodiac ruler. From House 1 to 12, they are activating the 12 signs of the zodiac. It is that natural ruler of the house that can also provide further insight. For instance, if Saturn is located in the 6th house of physical health and daily work, it is also activating the Virgo energy of that house (Virgo rules the 6th House because it is the 6th zodiac sign). Virgo is often an anxious energy that is looking to make sense out of the world. It can sometimes struggle with anxiety and obsessive compulsive disorder as it strives to understand all that it experiences. If Saturn (where life lessons are to be learned) were in this house, it would tell us that there would be lessons to be learned through physical health and learning to maintain order.

Following is a description of each of the houses, as they should be viewed for the outer planets. It takes into consideration the physical area that the house represents with the energy of its natural ruling sign. I recommend coming back to this area of the book after you complete the exercise. You will achieve a broad understanding of the placement of your outer planets while completing the exercise, but it is often in the details that we have our best insights. The table below will give you many insights on how to interpret the placement of your outer planets.

Exploring the Astrological Houses through the outer planets in the Natal Chart:

	MODE/ELEMENT	SIGN	ARCHETYPE	HOUSE ORIENTATION	NATURAL TALENTS	LIMITING BEHAVIORS	KEYWORDS
HOUSE 1	Cardinal Fire	Aries	The Warrior	Action Oriented	Independent & Confident	Aggressive & Overbearing	Physical Movement, Self, Appearance, View Point, Personality, Approach to Life

ACTIVATED SIGN

The energy of Aries in this house makes independence and individual self-expression a very important lesson to be mastered by this individual. They will crave experiences that are of an extreme nature to tap into the physicality of this world. There is a natural leadership quality to this energy and they have an amazing ability to generate ideas and motivate a crowd. However, just as quickly as they can generate ideas and create momentum, they can just as easily move on to the next thing – soon discovering that they have failed to see many of their ideas through to fruition.

	MODE/ELEMENT	SIGN	ARCHETYPE	HOUSE ORIENTATION	NATURAL TALENTS	LIMITING BEHAVIORS	KEYWORDS
HOUSE 2	Fixed Earth	Taurus	The Builder	Work Oriented	Dependable & Persistent	Stubborn & Stagnant	Values, Finances, Possessions, Investments, Movable Property, Money, The Senses

ACTIVATED SIGN

The energy of Taurus in this house makes the individual highly aware of their need to secure finances and solidify their values (a key lesson for their life). There can be some trouble managing personal finances because as much as they possess the potential to make money – they have equal potential to then go out and spend it. To help gain control of this cycle, it is imperative for this energy to have a savings account and to feel prepared. Ironically, when they have money in savings they are less likely to feel the urge to spend it.

	MODE/ELEMENT	SIGN	ARCHETYPE	HOUSE ORIENTATION	NATURAL TALENTS	LIMITING BEHAVIORS	KEYWORDS
HOUSE 3	Mutable Air	Gemini	The Storyteller	Relationship Oriented	Speaking & Curious mind	Gossip & Attention span	Sales, Verbal Communication, Early Education, Neighbors, Siblings, Short Trips

ACTIVATED SIGN

The energy of Gemini in this house creates a dynamic pull for communicating verbally with others. This individual will be naturally gifted with the ability to pitch ideas, create stimulating conversation and to have access to an endless amount of topics to talk about. In fact, this individual is known for their ability to talk to strangers (often they discover that strangers will share their life story with them during a first encounter). Without paying attention, they may find themselves gossiping and accidentally exaggerating to the point of telling a lie. It is best for this energy to keep a sharp awareness as to the details of the magnificent stories that they share (this will help prevent them from pushing the boundaries of truth too far).

	MODE/ELEMENT	SIGN	ARCHETYPE	HOUSE ORIENTATION	NATURAL TALENTS	LIMITING BEHAVIORS	KEYWORDS
HOUSE 4	Cardinal Water	Cancer	The Nurturer	Emotion Oriented	Intuitive & Caring	Projecting emotions & Fear of rejection	Family, Ancestry, Real Estate, Motherhood, Comfort, Food, Houses, Private

ACTIVATED SIGN

The energy of Cancer in this house pulls out a deeply intuitive individual with high Emotional Intelligence. There will be a constant insatiable need to connect with others emotionally. The natural care-giving quality of this house lends itself well to those in a position to care for others. With its roots tied to the home, ancestry and food - these things become of the utmost importance to the individual. This energy is known as the collector of the zodiac and throughout its life will be drawn to collecting. In the Outer World this can express as a need to collect objects, money, and trinkets. In the Inner World, there is a tendency to hang on to ideas, memories, and emotional trauma.

	MODE/ELEMENT	SIGN	ARCHETYPE	HOUSE ORIENTATION	NATURAL TALENTS	LIMITING BEHAVIORS	KEYWORDS
HOUSE 5	Fixed Fire	Leo	The Performer	Action Oriented	Performing & Creativity	Bossy & Patronizing	Children, Creative Arts, Engagement, Hobbies, Gambling, Pleasure, Taking Risks

ACTIVATED SIGN

The energy of Leo in this house enables an individual to tap into a limitless supply of creativity. They have a natural knack for performance and thrive when they can share their energy with others. Using their wit and charm, they act as a magnet to others and find it extremely easy to keep them engaged and laughing. There is a childlike quality to this energy, making them fun-loving spirits who are fantastic with children. Because they live for the reaction of others, they have a tendency to take things too far at times and can then become overly demanding.

	MODE/ELEMENT	SIGN	ARCHETYPE	HOUSE ORIENTATION	NATURAL TALENTS	LIMITING BEHAVIORS	KEYWORDS
HOUSE 6	Mutable Earth	Virgo	The Craftsman	Work Oriented	Intelligent and Engineering	Anxiety & Obsessive thought patterns	Daily Habits, Work, Co-Workers, Pets, Physical Health, Anxiety, Order

ACTIVATED SIGN

The energy of Virgo brings a unique perspective that allows a broad-minded approach to all endeavors. There is an opportunity to understand how things function and through this gift there is an ability to make things work more efficiently and more productively. This keen intellect will thrive in environments that are tidy and clean because they need to feel a sense of order in their physical environment. The ability to think at this level leaves this energy vulnerable to anxiety and obsessive-compulsive disorder. This is often times the right hand man, getting things done in a consistent and reliable manner.

	MODE/ELEMENT	SIGN	ARCHETYPE	HOUSE ORIENTATION	NATURAL TALENTS	LIMITING BEHAVIORS	KEYWORDS
HOUSE 7	Cardinal Air	Libra	The Peacemaker	Relationship Oriented	Sociable & Mediating	Avoidance & Decision making	Partnership, Relationships, Divorce, Legal, Art Appreciation, Architecture, Hearing

ACTIVATED SIGN

The energy of Libra in this house places an emphasis within the individual to grow through relationships. This is a naturally very popular individual who thrives on peacekeeping, mediating and seeing both sides. This energy always sees life in shades of grey and thus struggles when it comes to decision-making. It naturally will avoid conflict whenever possible and in some cases, this causes emotions to build up until they snap (this is why they are the great balancer of the zodiac). Finding the ability to blend with others in relationships while maintaining their own self-identity allows them to find the balance that they seek.

	MODE/ELEMENT	SIGN	ARCHETYPE	HOUSE ORIENTATION	NATURAL TALENTS	LIMITING BEHAVIORS	KEYWORDS
HOUSE 8	Fixed Water	Scorpio	The Alchemist	Emotion Oriented	Research & Charming personality	Possessive & Overly skeptical	Research, Other Peoples Money, Psychic, Wills, Sex, Death, Skepticism

ACTIVATED SIGN

The energy of Scorpio in this house lends a very mystical and transformative energy to the individual. The sign Scorpio is represented by two animals: the Scorpion and the Eagle. This is an extremely broad range and adds to the intensity experienced with Scorpio energy. It can express in low lows (the Scorpion) and high heights (The Eagle). It is the ruler of the gateway to the other side and therefore impacts birth, death, sex, intuition and psychic gifts. Charismatic and charming, they have a very powerful sexuality in their demeanor. They often want to feel in control and this has the potential to alienate those closest to them. Figuring out a way to put their powerful intuitive intellect to work on a specific purpose will make a huge difference in how their life evolves.

	MODE/ELEMENT	SIGN	ARCHETYPE	HOUSE ORIENTATION	NATURAL TALENTS	LIMITING BEHAVIORS	KEYWORDS
HOUSE 9	Mutable Fire	Sagittarius	The Philosopher	Action Oriented	Inspirational & Joyful	Avoiding responsibilities & Overthinking	Higher Education, Written Word, Travel, Philosophy, Literature, Religion

ACTIVATED SIGN

The energy of Sagittarius in this house creates a deep and endless desire for knowledge and exploration. There is an overflowing abundant nature to this person - they are the great philosophers who find they can take any subject and make it interesting. They thrive on new adventure, travel, reading and writing. Because they dream so big and crave so much greatness, this can cause an individual to shy away from daily life responsibilities. If not kept in check, this individual will most likely experience a bit of a Peter Pan syndrome – they won't want to grow up.

	MODE/ELEMENT	SIGN	ARCHETYPE	HOUSE ORIENTATION	NATURAL TALENTS	LIMITING BEHAVIORS	KEYWORDS
HOUSE 10	Cardinal Earth	Capricorn	The Entrepreneur	Work Oriented	Leadership & Persistence	Unreasonable expectations of others & Restless	Career, Public, Promotion, Fame, Father, Reputation, Social Status

ACTIVATED SIGN

The Capricorn energy in this house creates a commanding and goal oriented focus for the individual. There is a natural resilience of character and strong values are evident from a young age. This sign is truly the old soul at a young age and they subsequently grow more playful, young and fun loving as they age. Just like the sign Scorpio, there is a broad nature to this energy. It rules the lowest points of the Earth to the highest heights. They always see things through to fruition. There expectations of others are extremely high and they will have to learn over time how to be more realistic when it comes to the behaviors of others.

	MODE/ELEMENT	SIGN	ARCHETYPE	HOUSE ORIENTATION	NATURAL TALENTS	LIMITING BEHAVIORS	KEYWORDS
HOUSE 11	Fixed Air	Aquarius	The Inventor	Relationship Oriented	Teaching & Solving problems	Emotionally detached & Inability to relax	Innovation, Technology, Charity, Collective Vision, Step-Children, Community

ACTIVATED SIGN

The Aquarius energy is tapping into a deeper desire of moving humanity forward and up the evolutionary latter. From technology to world peace - this energy will push to see what it can achieve during their life-span. There is a natural teacher within this energetic expression because at the root of their being, they want to help elevate both the individual and the collective. In order to achieve its goal, they built in an emotional detachment that allows them to be the great problem-solvers of the zodiac. This very ability that helps them solve-problems works against them in personal relationship. They may find that they struggle to emotionally connect in romantic relationships and would do well to consciously push themselves to be just slightly more vulnerable.

	MODE/ELEMENT	SIGN	ARCHETYPE	HOUSE ORIENTATION	NATURAL TALENTS	LIMITING BEHAVIORS	KEYWORDS
HOUSE 12	Mutable Water	Pisces	The Artist	Emotion Oriented	Creativity & Intuition	Emotion Oriented	Art, Dreams, Faith, Film, Acting, Drugs, Escapism, Mental Health, Addiction

ACTIVATED SIGN

The Pisces energy of this house activates the need to connect with others through art and/or religion. This is a psychic house (all water houses have this tendency) and these individuals know a great deal about spirit. This powerful intuitive gift coupled with their ability to empathize makes this sign the most vulnerable energy in the zodiac. It is extremely important for this energy to master the balance between giving and taking. They want to provide service, but must learn to do this in a way that doesn't drain themselves of all their energy. There is an addictive tendency in this house for acts of escapism, simply due to the fact that they absorb far too much negativity from others into their psyche. They need to focus on restoring their reserve energy and taking care of themselves regularly and with great priority.

As you can see, each of the houses allows us to properly interpret the placement of these outer planets. We can look now at how the outer planets impacted the life of Michael Jackson. Jupiter, the planet of expansion and innate talent, was located in his 8th House. The 8th House corresponds to alchemy, research, psychic nature, and intuition. We also know that it is associated with the zodiac sign of Scorpio. Since Jupiter is expansive, we know that he would gain the gift of charm and charisma. In this specific case, because the energy of Scorpio is so broad, it opens the door to both the "high highs" and "low lows" (it is ruled by both the Eagle and the Scorpion). Michael did tap into the higher power of the Eagle's high highs, but unfortunately also had moments relating to the Scorpion's low lows.

Michael had Saturn in the 10th House (ruler of the public eye, career, and leadership). Saturn shows where the majority of his life lessons would be experienced and House 10 says that this would happen through his career and in front of the public. He started performing from a young age and essentially lost the opportunity to experience a typical childhood. Capricorn (ruler of House 10) is an energy that is "old when it is young" and "young when it is old." So much of Michael's life reflects that energy. No matter how much we may "make it" in this world, we are all still here learning new energy patterns and choosing the paths we take.

Uranus and Pluto were both located in House 6 (Virgo energy). Uranus indicates the areas where he would experience the unusual. We see by its placement that this would be happening through physical health and daily activities (House 6). Michael did suffer from some unusual health conditions. Pluto, teacher of tough lessons, was also showing that the majority of his spiritual growth would be learned through physical health and daily activities. Through his illness he was subjected to public ridicule and debate, and one would assume through that experience he was challenged internally and experienced some issues with his identity.

Astrology shows cycles—those cycles show the most probable time for events and circumstances to occur or unfold. When interpreting the information in your chart, keep in mind that we are looking at the themes and repeated patterns. Each chapter will reveal new insights, but you must put each of these insights together (just like a puzzle). It is you, and you alone, that has the most power on your journey and the greatest ability to put these pieces together. This is why I inevitably decided to write this book—my readings have always been powerful and insightful, but I believe you gain the most momentum, validation, and inspiration by claiming your own power and putting the puzzle together yourself. If you've ever watched someone put a puzzle together, you maybe smiled and acknowledged their accomplishments when they were complete. But, if you have ever put a complex puzzle together on your own—you know the moment that last piece finally fits into place, it creates a new sense of momentum and accomplishment within you that you had to earn yourself. Take your time putting these pieces together. Truly, you are remembering what your soul already knows, one piece at a time.

As you begin this exploration in your chart, please know that the outer planets are merely showing you how your outside environment could be interacting with you. It is up to you to choose how you manage these energies. We always have a choice to tap into the highest possible vibration of the sign or experience. With that ability, however, it opens the doorway for us to also tap into the lowest vibrations as well. As we continue to bring more and more free will into our human experience, we will see that our choices make all the difference. There is not just one big, giant choice you make in this life, but rather there are very many little choices that we make continuously that shape our destiny. Claim your power in these small choices so that you can subsequently claim your power on the big one. Consciously choose how your path will unfold where free will reigns. Consciously choose how you will react and respond when fate shows up.

Start Your Exercise!
THE INFLUENCES OF THE OUTER PLANETS

Gather valuable information on the function of your life and the choices you made before incarnating—discover where the majority of your life lessons will be learned.

See sample worksheet on page 117

EXERCISE
The Influences of the Outer Planets

In this exercise, you will begin to explore how the outer planets are influencing your life. Each house is numbered on the worksheet, The Influences of the Outer Planets. The area of life affected by each house is listed on the outermost portion of the circle. The archetype activated by house is listed on the inside of the circle. This exercise is designed to give you a brief overview of how these planets can be interpreted in your Natal Chart. Be sure to read more about the houses in the chapter to find out even more!

STEP 1:
Using your Natal Chart information, look to see where the social planets (Jupiter and Saturn) are located in your chart. Because these planets have a direct impact on your internal world, enter them into the inner portion of the circle on the worksheet. You will find this information in Table 1, Columns 1 and 4.

STEP 2:
Based on the location of Jupiter and Saturn, fill in the activated archetype and area of life (found in the rings of the circle) into the boxes below to discover what each of these planets is telling you in your Natal Chart.

STEP 3:
Now it is time to explore the remaining outer planets. Look to see where Uranus, Neptune, and Pluto are located in your Natal Chart. Enter their locations into the outermost portion of the circle to the right. You will find this information in Table 1, Columns 1 and 4.

STEP 4:
Based on the location of Uranus, Neptune, and Pluto, fill in the activated archetype and area of life (found in the rings of the circle) into the boxes below to discover what each of the planets is telling you in your Natal Chart.

CHAPTER 8
The Fortunes

POWER PLAN

- △ Understand the purpose behind our desire to incarnate onto the Earth plane
- △ Learn about The Part of Fortune and its ability to help align you with your path
- △ Piece together all of the concepts from Section 1 to create a concrete understanding of your life purpose

Accepting the concept of fate and our subsequent choice to come to Earth ultimately leads us to one perplexing question: Why would anyone incarnate into a life with less then desirable circumstances? When I put that question out into the non-physical world, it was answered immediately with another question from my spirit guides: What is the purpose of life? At first, I was shocked by such a short response from my guides who are always so eager to share with me all that they can. However, that question was the most powerful answer I could have been given.

Each individual spirit has a goal for their growth and that is why they chose to incarnate onto Earth. Based on their unique goal and purpose, a life is specifically crafted to help bring them to attainment of that goal. Sometimes the life that they incarnate into is met with much difficulty because the goal they are trying to reach requires those sets of circumstances. There are also karmic

responsibilities that many of us still have to work out and those circumstances and loose ends must be written into our lives (we must make right any of our wrongs).

Knowing that coming to Earth is just like enrolling in school: we don't always enjoy each and every class that we take, but sometimes it is part of our curriculum. The experience of a difficult life is creating a dynamic circumstance for the potential of growth that was important to you on the other side. During our human existence, we experience time in specific linear format: past, present, and future. However, we do not experience time in that same fashion on the other side. Where time appears to stretch out and linger here—it is happening very quickly on the other side.

Once I fully digested that information, it validated my deeper knowing of how important it is for people to understand their unique life mission and aim. The truth is that just because we incarnated, it doesn't mean that we will ultimately attain our goals. We have to rise to the circumstances and harness the power of free will and fate to realize that which we set out to do. Luckily, there are various tools available to help us explore what our purpose is. I believe that astrology has the potential to be one of the strongest and most accurate of these tools (if you use the right birth time). Its ability to bridge science with spirit astounds me every day. By learning and exploring all that you can in your Natal Chart, you gain the opportunity to understand that goal you had when you made the choice to incarnate. This knowledge is sacred and should be treated as such. When you experience the validation that the stars have to offer, it can catapult you in the direction of your life purpose in a way you never expected.

Part of the difficulty of incarnating is that we forget much of everything we experienced in our past lives. On top of that, the majority of us also forget the fact that we are truly eternal non-physical beings. However, if these circumstances were reversed and we remembered everything, it would inevitably have consequences on the life you are living. If you have ever gone to see a movie after reading about the plot, you know that the experience of viewing the movie has inextricably been altered. Knowing the plot in advance may have given you a sense of control, but the emotional response and impact you would have had was then changed in some way. The beauty of astrology is that it provides us with enough insight to help validate our life purpose, without telling us every detail of how it will unfold. Therefore, we can actively participate and experience the joy of living and reaching our goals authentically.

In astrology, there are various sensitive points that can be calculated in your Natal Chart, referred to as "The Fortunes." These are ancient mathematical calculations that use the specific location of your planets at the moment of your birth to calculate further insights into your life purpose. The Part of Fortune is the most popular of these mathematical calculations that can enable us to gain further insight. It acts more like a symbol than any of the other planets and sheds light onto what it is that you deeply desire or want. It is the light at the

end of the tunnel, so to speak, and it was created to help guide you to align with your purpose and aim for this life.

Based on its location in your chart, you will be able to validate the deeper burning desire that you have always felt within. The exercise at the end of this chapter will help you discover how that "want" is contributing to your overall goal in this life. Piece by piece, we will bring together all of the concepts we have explored to paint a vivid picture of what your life is about. Tying the pieces together is the key to unlocking the potential of your life. This portion of astrology is truly the most validating—much of this you may have already known deep within, but perhaps you did not have the confidence or belief to know your life has purpose.

Thomas Edison is one of the most fascinating individuals who has incarnated on Earth. Here was a young man who only had three months of official schooling, yet he went on to hold 1,093 US patents in his name. He created things that no one dared to dream existed. How did he do it? How did he chart his life so that he could realize his potential? And of course, how can we do the same? The answer does not lie solely with The Part of Fortune (that would be too easy). It is the culmination of all of the concepts we have already explored, and it is now time to put it all together.

Thomas Edison was strongest in the air element (6 planets), which made him highly intellectual and gave him an ability to see the big picture. His modes had a rather equal distribution of 4 (Cardinal), 6 (Fixed) and 6 (Mutable). This shows his ability to come up with an idea, see it through, and to bend like the wind when needed. He also had a major Power Cluster of 5 planets in the House of Curiosity and Communication (House 3)! Three of these five planets were inner planets: Sun, Mercury, and Venus. One was a social planet: Saturn. And the last one was an outer planet: Neptune. The Sun (ego expression) and Mercury (mind) were both in the sign of Aquarius (The Inventor). His Moon (instinctual self) was in Sagittarius, the sign of The Philosopher.

Edison's South Moon Node was in the 2nd quadrant (private, personal, and family) and his North Node was in the 4th quadrant (the public and professional). His life was all about becoming a leader and going public. More specifically, his North Node was in House 11, the House of Invention and challenging the status quo. His pull in this life was to come up with new ideas and better ways of doing things. And right there next to his North Node in House 10 was his Part of Fortune.

With this sensitive point being in the 10th House, we know that there was a deep desire to be before the public and to be recognized by the masses. Edison's desire to be seen in this light nudged him forward. This was "the something" he wanted. He had all the energetic makeup to become an inventor, but it was "that need" to be seen that assisted him. He didn't just automatically come up with inventions; it took hard work and perseverance to bring these things into existence. The light bulb, phonograph, and carbon microphone didn't just appear out of thin air! It took dedication and focus to see them through and, because of where his Part of Fortune was located, I believe the reason he got such a kick out of making these things happen was for the public's reaction. He was earning his spot in the public eye.

The placement of The Part of Fortune is calculated by the Ascendant + Moon – Sun. It shows a sensitive point in your chart and often a sensitive point in your life. It is one of the most powerful signposts that can lead you to align with your Moon Nodes and your life aim. The house and sign that The Part of Fortune occupies is the key to how you will decipher its meaning.

Edison had 27°Scorpio as his Ascendant. We know that his personal power phrase was, "I Desire." The two planets ruling his chart are Pluto and the Moon. He had Pluto located in Aries (The Warrior) in House 5 (The House of Creativity). The Moon was located in Sagittarius (The Philosopher) in House 2 (The House of Finances and Values). We know that his desire was to act as a Warrior and create to help feed his philosophical mind and wallet. It is this aim, coupled with The Nodes and The Part of Fortune that are always working together to help you harness the potential you brought into this life.

Once you have completed the next exercise, you will have uncovered what it is that you "want"

in this life. You will be able to piece together the information from the other chapters to create a solidified understanding of your purpose here on Earth. Claiming your power to be all that you can be is your number one responsibility in this life. It is an interesting thing, power. It has the ability to transform itself into a vast amount of experiences, people and places. Power in its true essence is energy, just like everything else in this Universe. When we are claiming our power, we are guiding our path through our own divine essence. When we are not claiming our power, we are allowing our own essence to be guided by the forces outside of us. This is often seen when one blindly follows an "authority" figure or a person, event or circumstance outside of oneself (while ignoring their own internal voice).

Many many moons ago, I was a manager at a very high-sales retail store with a ton of visibility. I was being supported by an individual who was my "authority" figure in the company. On the surface, she was extremely successful and had risen quickly. When viewing her based on her position and rank in this company, I felt (at the time) that her guidance and support should essentially trump my own inner guidance and support.

There were a million and one signs from the Universe that I needed to claim my power and not blindly follow her lead, BUT I didn't have faith yet in my ability to lead and manage my team. The first indication came during a staff meeting when she interrupted me and took over the whole meeting. During that process, she was extremely tough and approached the team from a leadership style rooted in fear. She even told my staff (against the company code of conduct), that if they were to call in sick even once, they needed to provide a doctor's note or they would lose their jobs.

You would think in that moment where I myself KNEW that it went against the company code of conduct that I would have spoken up, doubted her, and risen into my own personal power. I didn't. She took me aside after that meeting and explained to me why she needed to take control of the meeting (because I clearly "wasn't demanding respect" from my team). She told me that if my staff didn't fear me, I would never be a successful manager. I cried and knew deep in my heart that there was another way to lead, nurture, and grow a successful team rooted through compassion and support. I ignored my own power and allowed hers to guide me.

The Universe often gives us a lot of opportunities to guide our own path, but sometimes for whatever reason, we shy away from them—afraid to trust our own instincts, our own voice. During times like these, it is often the great poignant moments that actually allow us to dig deep within ourselves and force us to reclaim our power. That was absolutely how the path was unfolding for me in this situation.

I had just finished up the holiday season and needed to deliver some difficult news to the seasonal employees. I would be deciding who would be staying on the team in a permanent position and who I would have to let go. There were roughly twenty-five to thirty seasonal employees on my team at that time. Typically, the end of the holiday season for seasonal employees is pretty straightforward—their contract ends. The issue with that particular season was that I was a new manager and made a pivotal error. I told the holiday hires that they had the opportunity to stay on after the holiday season (thinking that would be a type of motivation). The problem to my approach was that I was unable to keep every single employee on AND the majority of the employees wanted to stay (I didn't think that would happen). So you see, I had created a conundrum where virtually all of the holiday employees had the expectation they would be transitioning onto the team. It was indeed a very tense time for me and I was heart-broken over the circumstance that I had accidentally created. I was embarrassed and ashamed, I felt lost and didn't know how to fix the situation I'd created.

When I was discussing the process of how to handle this with the "authority" figure, she negated my plan to talk to them one on one. She told me that I didn't have enough time and that I would need to schedule two meetings back to back; one meeting where I would let them know they were going to be staying on the team and one where I would let them all go.

Yes, I was to hold a meeting where I essentially let go or "fired" roughly ten staff at once. Like I said, I had created the circumstance through my own inexperience and misguided notion (not realizing that everyone who "performed" would expect to transition onto the team). My stomach churned over the disrespectful energy that was infused in such a meeting. I respected those staff and wanted them to know that I hadn't come to the decision lightly, that I valued their hard work through the holiday season, and that I would love for them to reapply in the future. I knew in my heart that speaking to them in a group format about their employment stripped the dignity out of the process and their experience with our company.

Going against my gut, I held that meeting. The "authority" figure was right there by my side, telling me that I was being a more efficient manager and a stronger person. I choked out the words in that meeting and let them all go (from their perspective, I had fired them). One girl lost it and started crying and shouting at me. I don't blame her—she had every right.

There are not many moments in my life where I've felt truly ashamed of an action I took. I feel truly ashamed that I followed blindly and didn't claim my power in that moment. I could have made time to meet with each one of those staff for ten minutes each and connect in with them—explain the circumstance and thank them for their commitment to the job. Rather then following that path, I had just blindly followed someone else's guidance system and ignored my own.

Right after that meeting I went to the bathroom and vomited. I couldn't believe who I was becoming, and I knew that I had followed the path blindly and not listened to my own inner guidance. This is what I mean when I say it's time to claim your power. It's time to listen to your own internal voice and choose the path that lights you up, brightens your soul, and FEELS right in your heart. It's time to trust your intuition, your gut, and follow YOUR path.

The truth is that the method the "authority" figure was using worked for her. She wasn't coming from the wrong place because that method was a part of her path, her evolution, and her way to grow. The trouble wasn't in how she approached the situation. The trouble was in the fact that I ignored my own internal guidance and followed a path that would NEVER work for me.

Even if an "authority" figure has risen to such a level in their consciousness that they were completely heart-focused, I still do not believe that any individual should hand their power (their essence) over to them entirely. I don't believe we should silence our own inner voice until the point where we forget who we are and transform into a person we are not.

Claiming your power isn't about discrediting someone else's path, judging it, or trying to derail it. Claiming your power is birthed from within you and is rooted in faith and belief of the evolution of your own essence, when at the same time you have faith and belief in the evolutionary path unfolding for every other soul in this world. You see, there is a greater intelligence running through all of us (call it God or Great Spirit or whatever word suits your beliefs) and your only job is to connect in with your own voice and essence and follow YOUR path. The true inner voice is rooted in love, acceptance, and compassion. Claiming your power is both complete liberation and complete surrender to a force and energy much larger than yourself.

My story of claiming my power has happened again and again. In that scenario, I reported the behavior and transferred to another store (a decision that seemed like a back step, but actually catapulted me into a much better scenario where I achieved massive success in alignment with my values). We are always being tested to claim our power, follow our intuition, and steer the course of our lives. I soon claimed my power in that situation, led from my heart, had record-breaking sales, and took on my own self-created management style: Intuitive Leadership.

Consciousness is always expanding and I have had an ever-evolving array of experiences presented that allowed me to understand the importance of claiming my power. You see, the process of claiming your power (your essence) is about calling back your energy and living authentically through your heart.

One of the reasons I wrote this book was because of the power I see handed over to astrologers, psychics, and intuitives. There is so much beauty and awareness that is birthed through astrology, but exploring the Natal Chart is something that I believe should empower the individual to discover and validate their very essence—their very power. It is sacred; your chart belongs to you. Every reading I do honors this, and I know that any wisdom that comes through me must also connect in with you to be valid to your path (your voice, your path).

When you complete this exercise, I will prompt you to claim your power. I sincerely hope that you carry this in your heart because we don't get to just claim our power once and continue down the path. We will constantly need to re-claim our power, follow our guidance, and rise up to be the person we were born to be.

Start Your Exercise!
THE FORTUNES

Piece together all the information you have decoded in the previous exercises—gain the awareness needed to understand yourself though the cosmic perspective.

EXERCISE
The Fortunes

In this exercise we will finally be able to put all of the pieces of the puzzle together. We will journey back through the information we discovered in previous exercises to gain full clarity. We will see how all that was revealed to us through our Natal Chart fits together.

STEP 1:

1. Looking back to chapter 3 and the Divine Life Purpose: Uncovering the Mystery of your Moon Nodes worksheet, enter your South and North Moon Nodes into the circle on The Fortunes worksheet.

2. Draw an arrow from the South Moon Node to the North Node to indicate the direction of this current incarnation.

STEP 2:

Looking back to chapter 5, enter your specific life aim into the middle of the circle.

STEP 3:

1. Using the information on your Natal Chart Navigator, determine the house that your Part of Fortune is located in.

2. Write your Part of Fortune into the big circle on the worksheet.

3. Look to see the house and archetype activated by its location to determine what you "want" in this life.

4. Once you specify this "want" write it into the box below the circle.

STEP 4:

1. You should have a firm understanding of the spiritual direction you anticipated for this current incarnation. We will now look to see how you are going to achieve this. To determine the amount of fate and free will that you are working with, look back to chapter 2.

2. Enter the number of planets from the left side of your chart into the Free Will box.

3. Enter the number of planets on the right side of your chart into the Fate box.

STEP 5:

1. To understand the gifts you chose prior to this incarnation to assist you in achieving this goal, look to the Elements and Modes worksheet in chapter 1 to determine the most dominant element and mode in your chart.

2. Check the circle or triangle that applies. If there was a tie, check both. The gift of that element and mode is noted below the circles.

STEP 6:

Now we will determine the aspects of your personality that you chose prior to incarnating to support you on your path. Looking back to chapter 4, enter the three most dominant archetypes from your personality to discover your greatest gifts.

Now claim your power.

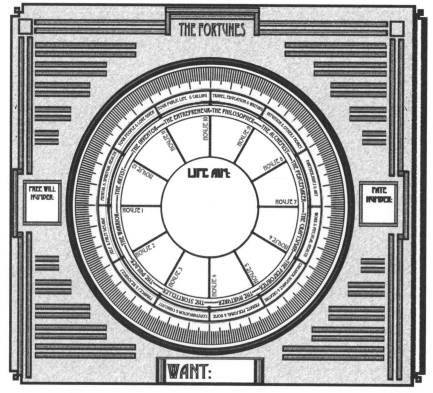

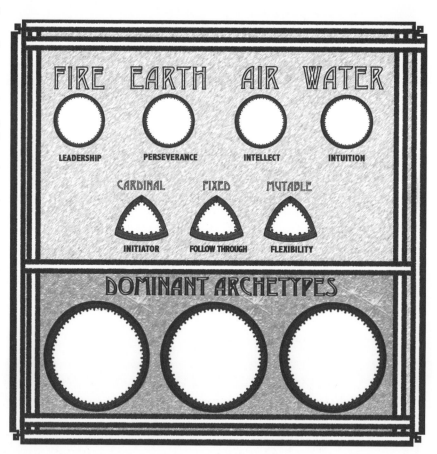

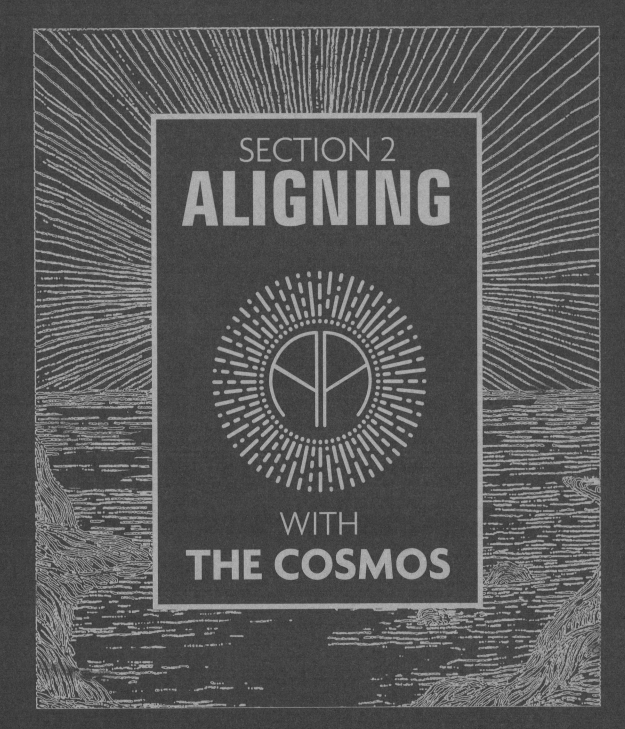

SECTION 2
ALIGNING

WITH
THE COSMOS

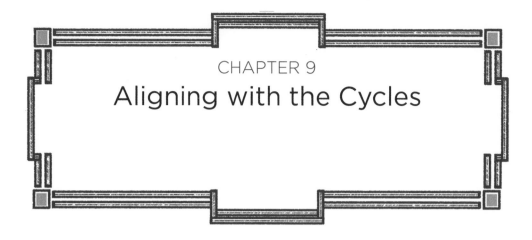

CHAPTER 9

Aligning with the Cycles

POWER PLAN

△ Learn how the transiting planets affect how our lives develop by their cyclical nature

△ Determine the three main considerations when using predictive astrology

△ Understand retrograde motion and how it uniquely affects your life by the houses

There is nothing more exciting in astrology than its innate ability to help you see into the future. So far within this workbook, we have primarily been concerned with your Natal/Birth Chart and where the planets were located at the exact moment of your birth. These planets, of course, never stop moving and are merely captured at the moment of your arrival—providing the static image astrologers use in the Natal Chart. As the planets continue to move in their cycles, they move throughout your chart for the rest of your life. This consistent pattern allows us the unique ability to see how events, situations, and relationships will inevitably develop and grow throughout our lives.

Each planet will move in a counter-clockwise direction after your birth and progress through the Houses numerically: from House 1 to House 2, so forth and so on. If you have ever had a professional Natal Chart Reading, you will see that the current planet locations are recorded on the outermost

portion of your chart. This continued movement of the planets is referred to as "transits." When someone says, "Mars is transiting your 6th House," they are saying that regardless of its location at the moment of your birth, it is currently activating your 6th House. In Table 3 of your Natal Chart Navigator, you will be able to view each of the planets' current location in the Houses.

There are a few things to keep in mind when it comes to understanding how the planets will continue their journey. The first point is that each planet will travel through your chart at a specific rate of speed, some slowly and others much faster. The farther the planets are away from the Sun, the longer the journey around your Natal Chart (some will only make it through a few houses in your lifetime). As we discovered in Section 1, the inner planets reflect things that happen inside of us. This also means that the transiting influences of these planets: Sun, Moon, Mercury, Venus, and Mars will be helpful, generally speaking, in predicting our internal evolution. The social planets, just as we have already explored, show their influences on both the internal and external level and thus help predict on both levels—internally and externally. The remaining outer planets: Uranus, Neptune, and Pluto, due to the length of time it takes them to pass through each sign, have a generational effect on us collectively as a whole. (I would like to quickly note, however, that the movement of an outer planet into a new house in your chart, would make an impact in your life).

The next point to note regarding transiting planets is how the degrees of the zodiac fit into your specific astrological houses. Remember, each chart is unique and how the signs are distributed into the houses is dependent on your birth information. Transits are looking at where the planets are in the zodiac right now, at this very moment. If Mars were currently in the sign of Scorpio, it would be in the sign of Scorpio for everyone else as well. Knowing Mars is in Scorpio can help us gain a general sense of the planetary influence on a mass consciousness level, but we gain even more clarity of its effects in our lives based on the house it is traveling through in our chart. This means that when we look at transits, although the sign the planet is in does matter, the main question we need to immediately ask ourselves is, "What house is this planet currently transiting in my chart?"

More often than not, the astrological houses don't correspond perfectly to the 30 degrees of each sign in the zodiac; sometimes there can be more than 30 degrees in a house and sometimes less. In all cases, however, there will always be 180 degrees, of the 360-degree zodiac, covering the bottom and top portions of the Natal Chart. This is easy to ascertain, as the Ascendant will always mark the degree and sign of the 1st House. On the opposite side of the circle, The Descendant marks the start of the 7th House. The Descendant is always the same degree and opposite sign of your Ascendant—cutting the zodiac in half and putting 180 degrees above and below the circle in your Natal Chart. If you had 15°Aries for your Ascendant/Rising Sign, then you will inevitably have 15°Libra for your Descendant (Libra is opposite of Aries in the zodiac).

The Ascendant represents how others experience you and your general approach to life. The Descendant reflects a deeper part of who you are and is often reflective of who people come to know after they have become intricately woven into your life. It is a more vulnerable energy of your personality because it is uniquely connected to your Ascendant (because it is the opposite sign and the flip-side of the coin so to speak). The Descendant exists deep within the personality, but that part is something that is often shielded from the world and from others upon first impressions.

Each house will be ruled by one, two, or three signs of the zodiac specific to you. The house cusps mark the beginning of each house and have a specific sign and degree unique to you (see Table 2 of your Natal Chart Navigator). If you discover that you have a house with three signs represented, this is referred to as an Intercepted Chart. When this happens, the movement of the transiting planets through the Houses may be slightly longer in the houses with three signs. This means that the planet will move more quickly through the houses with only one sign to make up the difference. When you generated your Natal Chart Navigator, it pulled the transits for that specific time that you ran the report. If you would like the most precise interpretation of your transits, I recommend rerunning the Natal Chart Navigator again so that you have the precise locations when you complete these exercises.

The last remaining point to discuss regarding transits is the impact of retrograde motion. There are times when a planet may appear to move backwards in the sky based on its location relative to the Earth. This illusion of the planet moving backwards is termed "retrograde" and happens to more planets than just Mercury. Retrograde motion impacts how the transiting planet takes their journey around your chart. If the planet was in House 8 when it turned retrograde, it will then be activating the 8th House for a longer duration of time. Retrograde motion has an inward pull and is often asking us to slow down and contemplate our actions. With this slowing down, the planet then has an extended stay in the house it is transiting—it will create a dynamic impact in that area of your life.

My mentor, Nancy, explained this concept to me perfectly. She asked me to imagine that there was a circular pool and everyone was moving in the same direction clockwise on the outermost portion of the pool. By moving together in that direction, there would eventually be a pull that was created within the water assisting in pushing them forward. Then she asked me to imagine that everyone all of a sudden stopped and changed directions. Inevitably, the force that was created moving clockwise, would work against them as they initially changed directions to counter-clockwise. This is precisely how we experience the time periods when a planet goes retrograde. The toughest part of the retrograde period is aligning with the new direction that the energy is pulling us in. This is why so often there are distractions, disturbances, and miscommunication when a planet turns retrograde. An important fact to note, the impact of retrograde motion actually begins to take effect on us just before the illusion begins, by roughly one to two weeks.

Without a doubt, Mercury Retrograde has become highly popularized and noticeably impactful on our lives for a very important reason—this is due to the integral nature communication plays in our daily lives. Mercury is known as "the messenger" and rules communication and learning. When the energy shifts in this opposite direction, we stumble and often find ourselves frustrated and agitated without knowing why. When Mercury turns retrograde (which it does typically three to four times a year), this planet will inevitably be in one of the 12 houses of your chart. If Mercury turned retrograde when it was transiting your 7th House, ruling partnerships, the retrograde energy would most likely affect relationships in your life. If Mercury were transiting your 10th House, which rules career calling, the energy would most likely be experienced at work. For me personally, just understanding the "why" behind certain changes in my life allows me to relax and claim my power. Wouldn't it be nice to know what house Mercury is transiting in your chart when it turns retrograde? Astrology truly is a gift that never stops giving and all we have to do is listen, watch, and learn.

All of the points mentioned prior should be considered when you work with predictive astrology: the speed in which a planet travels through the zodiac, your specific distribution of the zodiac into the houses, and retrograde motion. Because this area of astrology is so powerful, I recommend that you continuously watch and choose to align with the transiting planets in your chart. There is much to be explored when it comes to the predictive nature of astrology. (In this book, we will be looking at the transits of Jupiter and Saturn in depth. In this first transit exercise, we will begin by first understanding the general impact occurring with all of the transiting planets.)

Just as we began exploring the Natal Chart through element and mode, we will do this now through the lens of the transiting planets. Please look at the date for the transits at the top of your Natal Chart Navigator (if it is off by more than three days, I suggest going online to download one that is up to date with the current location of the planets: www.absolutelyastrology.com). Get ready! This is where astrology really begins to take off— providing you now with the power to consciously align yourself with the cosmos!

Start Your Exercise!
ALIGNING WITH THE CYCLES

Take your first glimpse at how predictive astrology can help guide you into consciously aligning with the cosmos.

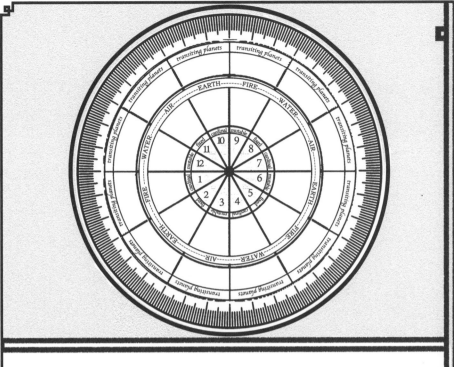

See sample worksheet on page 119

◦ELEMENT◦

FIRE:
spiritual, birthing, beginnings, leadership, confidence, ego development, aggression, physical movement.

EARTH:
securing resources, grounding, efficiency, livelihood, finances, career, roots, stability, home.

AIR:
learning, communication, socializing, new activities, broad perspective, debating, philosophizing.

WATER:
emotional, connection, intuitive, breaking through limitations, time for releasing emotional pain.

◦MODE◦

CARDINAL:
this is a time for action.

FIXED:
this is a time for persistence.

MUTABLE:
this is a time to bend with the wind.

◦FORECAST◦

◦ELEMENT◦

◦MODE◦

EXERCISE
Aligning with the Cycles

STEP 1:

In Table 3 of your Natal Chart Navigator, you will be able to determine the house that each planet is currently transiting in your chart. On the blank outermost portion of the circle on the Aligning with the Cycles worksheet, write each of the transiting planets' location into the appropriate houses. If a planet is currently retrograde, it will be noted next to the planet name in Table 3. If the planet is retrograde, write "Rx" next to its name. Use the key below to help you keep track of the planets you've marked.

☐ sun ☐ mercury ☐ mars ☐ saturn ☐ neptune
☐ moon ☐ venus ☐ jupiter ☐ uranus ☐ pluto

STEP 2:

1. Add up the total number of planets in each house.

2. Write this number into the blank inner segment circle. Notice the element and mode activated in each house as you enter the number.

STEP 3:

Each house, just like each zodiac sign, is represented by an element and mode. For each of the 12 houses, the element and mode have been written into the worksheet. Each of the elements and a short description is written in the column to the right of the circle on the worksheet.

1. Add the total numbers for each element: Fire, Earth, Air, and Water and write them next to the element name in the right hand column.

2. Also do this for the modes: Cardinal, Fixed, and Mutable.

STEP 4:

By determining the element and mode that are most dominant, you will be able to decipher the current "weather" forecast for your life.

1. Pick three words from the most dominant element definition and enter them into the "Forecast" portion to the right.

2. Just below that, you will enter the phrase associated with your most dominant mode. If there is a tie between two elements or modes, write both down in the "Forecast."

As we continue to discover how the forces of the unseen are influencing your life, keep these insights in mind.

CHAPTER 10
Taking Flight with Saturn

POWER PLAN

○ Discover the power behind the Saturn Transit and its influence over career, marriage, and all social happenings
○ Learn the four distinct phases of the Saturn Transit: Take Off and Climb, Cruising Altitude, Initial Descent, and Landing
○ Determine the influence Saturn currently has over your life and how to align with that phase

Of all the transits, Saturn has the most powerful position in our Universe. It rules over some of the things we, in our human experience, have come to value as high on our "to do" list. From marriage to career, if there is a social or political nature involved, leave it to Saturn to decide both the time and the manner that those areas of your life will or won't develop. During the 29.5 years it takes Saturn to complete its cycle, it will move through the four quadrants of your Natal Chart, spending roughly 7.5 years in each. Remember, Natal Saturn is where the planet was at the moment of your birth. Based on its natal position in your chart, you jumped in at one of these four phases of the Saturn Transit. As time proceeded on, Transiting Saturn continued to move through each phase and provide structure to your life.

This transit is very logical and easy to follow. If you divide a Natal Chart into four quadrants (by splitting it both horizontally and vertically), this illustrates the four distinct phases of the Saturn transit. The natural

starting point for the Saturn cycle begins at the lowermost point of the Natal Chart and correlates with the beginning of House 4. The 4th, 7th, 10th, and 1st Houses mark the starting point of each quadrant and have a natural rhythm, which we will learn about in depth within this chapter. Remember, the transiting planets are always moving in a counter-clockwise direction around your Natal Chart (unless the planet is retrograde; then it moves backwards). Since strict Saturn wouldn't want us to beat around the bush, let's jump right in and see what insight each of the phases within its cycle can provide. To help you build a solid understanding of how this transit works, we will view the journey Saturn takes around your chart through the lens of a plane flight. The four phases are:

1. Take Off and Climb
2. Cruising Altitude
3. Final Descent
4. Landing

Phase 1: Take Off and Climb
(Saturn Transit enters your 4th House)

This is the natural starting point for the Saturn cycle, just as it is the natural starting phase of any flight you will ever take: Take off and Climb. During this phase, you are eager and feel a sense of motion forward and up! This is a powerful new experience and in this leg of the journey, you are "elevating" your status and hitting new heights. Emotionally, you become filled with a sense of purpose and destiny. . . you know where you are going (that final destination is clear)! You've found a new direction and you are committed. It's as if, when Saturn begins its transit through your 4th House and begins Phase 1, your life starts happening. All that hard work on the job finally pays off—and you finally receive the recognition from those around you that you rightfully deserve. Perhaps you meet someone who connects you with a new career opportunity or you find yourself entering a new relationship or union. This is about starting a new journey and can manifest in marriage, career, or relocation. If you were already in a stable career or marriage, get ready! You may be "upgrading" the one you have or find yourself a whole lot more fortunate and joyful with that current person.

Phase 2: Cruising Altitude
(Saturn Transit enters your 7th House)

After you've made that initial climb and reached new heights, you're ready to coast and make serious progress on your journey. When you hit Phase 2, you have officially arrived at Cruising Altitude. This portion of the Saturn Transit is all about covering ground and making headway in life. In fact, during the roughly 7.5 years Saturn spends in this phase, you will feel like you have made more "progress" in your life than during any other time. With Saturn's entry into your 7th House, that new job or marriage you started back at the beginning of Phase 1 will receive new opportunities, promotions, and advancements. The year Saturn will spend at the tiptop of your chart (right before entering Phase 3) is typically the year when everything comes together for you. As you begin to approach your final destination there is a culminating life event or experience (think promotion, marriage, or children), right as Saturn makes his entry into your 10th House.

Phase 3: Final Descent
(Saturn Transit enters your 10th House)

As Saturn hits the highest point in your chart (in the beginning of House 10) you will enter Phase 3: Final Descent. This is a preparatory phase and one where you tie up loose ends. In flight, they announce that your final destination is in sight and it is time to put away your belongings and prepare for landing. Although no one will be announcing over an intercom that your life will be entering your Final Descent, you intuitively will begin to feel a need to prepare and take inventory of your belongings. This is when you finally do all the things on your priority list that you hadn't gotten to yet: meet with your financial advisor, prepare legal documents, or purchase a home. Your actions are about longevity at this point and preparing for the long haul. You feel a sense of obligation to prepare and get your "ducks in a row."

Phase 4: Landing
(Saturn Transit enters your 1st House)

Now you've landed, but you can't get off that plane! This is the most frustrating phase of the Saturn transit because, let's face it, you're stuck on that plane until someone opens the door and allows you to exit. All of that excitement and preparation has culminated in this leg of the journey where you are coasting on the runway. You have to wait on "other people" to make things happen in your life, and although you feel a sense of urgency to get on with things, the physical world does not have that same level of urgency. You are focusing on all the steps you will take once the door opens (much emphasis here on future actions) and there is a feeling that life is running in slow motion—all of a sudden you have entered a waiting period. You're waiting to get off the plane, you're waiting to get your luggage, you're waiting to get a taxi or picked up at the airport, you're waiting to arrive at your hotel. You are waiting! This is truly a holding pattern and time of self-reflection and introspection as Saturn begins transiting through, Phase 4: Landing, in your chart.

As you wait, it dawns on you that you have finally arrived at a specific destination! Believe it or not, the action you took and the decisions you made all the way back in Saturn's natural starting point of Phase 1, are exactly the very actions that brought you to this final destination. Now the tough part begins. Did all of your actions and intentions from those initial two phases have you arrive at a fulfilling destination? If yes, well done to you! You will feel a deep sense of gratification and satisfaction and eagerly accept this seven-year time of rest. If no, this will be the hardest seven years of your life. During this time, no matter the amount of action you take, your results will not be met with the same level for your efforts. As frustrating as this time can be for some, despair not, for Saturn is without a doubt the most consistent planet and cycle of astrology. Your time will come again to take flight—and this time you can consciously choose your destination!

It came as no surprise to my mentor, Nancy, that the Saturn Transit was and still is one of my favorite parts of astrology. Being an eternal realist and a lover of truth and honesty, I immediately loved the raw, blunt power of the Saturn Transit in our lives. It made sense, was easy to follow, and was always accurate. With Capricorn Rising, I of course have a kinship with Saturn, because after all, it is my Ruling Planet. I see things in black and white, right versus wrong, and Saturn operates much like that—straight and to the point: determining when you'll get that promotion at work or when you will get married . . . (successfully)!

As you can see, there is a natural rhythm to the Saturn transit and it is very easy to follow once you get the hang of it. As each of these phases unfolds: Take Off and Climb, Cruising Altitude, Final Descent, and Landing you will experience events and circumstances that validate this transit in your life. In this exercise, we will take a look at which phase you entered in at the time of your birth, and which phase you are currently in according to its transiting location. For many, this will be an incredibly validating experience! I have had many readings where I've sat with an individual who was leaving the landing phase of Saturn and they felt like a weight had been lifted off their shoulders! The confusion many experience during that particular phase is always very intense—their logical brain struggles to grasp why their life wasn't moving forward as expected.

When you begin working with the Saturn transit in your life, keep in mind that the right side of your chart, Phase 1: Take Off and Climb and Phase 2: Cruising Altitude, are a time of action in your life. This is when things are really happening and your level of output will be met with the same level, if not more, of input. However, as Saturn Transits the left side of your chart, Phase 3: Final Descent, and especially Phase 4: Landing, you are being called to the inward journey. Do not make the mistake of harboring feelings of dislike towards the inward journey. Just as you make movement forward in the physical world when Saturn transits the right side of your chart, you make movement forward spiritually as Saturn transits the left side of your chart. The physical manifestations of your life slow down when Saturn journeys down the left-hand side of your chart, providing an opportunity for your internal growth, understanding, and acceptance. You can also interpret Saturn's journey up and through the right side of the chart (phases: take off and climb and cruising altitude) as a time of acquiring and gathering in the physical world. On the flip-side, Saturn's journey down the left side of the chart (phases: final descent and landing) is a time of release and purging of that what no longer serves. And isn't that why we incarnated in the first place?

There is a bonus portion to the exercise that will allow you to calculate the four pivotal points of the Saturn cycle in your chart. As Saturn enters your 4th, 7th, 10th, and 1st House you will begin one of its four phases. As Saturn enters these specific turning points in your chart, you will be starting one of the four phases: take off and climb, cruising altitude, final descent and landing. Saturn has one of the longer orbits because it takes roughly 29.5 years to travel through the zodiac (which means it takes roughly 29.5 years to travel around your chart). Seeing as we spend about 7.5 years in each phase, it can be very powerful to understand when these phase changes are happening in your life.

I have found that the impact of Saturn is deeply felt within its journey through the houses and how that reflects to the activation of the 4 phases. In fact, if you like the Saturn transit, you can dive deeply into this influence in Grant Lewi's book *Astrology for the Millions*. The bonus section will allow you to identify the exact degree when Saturn enters the new phase (based on the sign that it is in).

As we have learned, everyone's chart is different and what marks Saturn's journey into your 4th House will inevitably be different than another's. Through the exercise, you will determine what degree and sign Saturn will be in when it moves into a new phase in your life. Saturn moves through the zodiac roughly every 29.5 years from: Aries to Taurus, Gemini to Cancer, Leo to Virgo, Libra to Scorpio,

Sagittarius to Capricorn, and Aquarius to Pisces. If you are currently in Phase 4: Landing, it would be wise indeed to watch the current planetary positions to determine when Saturn will enter your 4th House and begin Phase 1: Take Off and Climb. For instance, if you determined your 4th House begins at 4°Taurus, the moment that Saturn is at 4°Taurus, it is entering Phase 1: Take Off and Climb in your life. If planning to launch a business or start a new venture, if you can time it with Phase 1 of this transit (rather than Phase 4), you will be consciously aligning with the cosmos—and thus receiving the benefit of a more fortuitous start. You can always view the current planetary positions at www.absolutelyastrology.com to keep up with the cosmic movements.

This is also true for all of the phase changes Saturn will take in your life. I specifically recommend that you pay particular attention to when Saturn moves from Phase 3: Final Descent, to Phase 4: Landing. As you are well aware at this point, Phase 4: Landing, is definitely a holding pattern and waiting period for your life on the physical plane. Knowing when you will enter this phase might just be the fuel you need to tie up those loose ends and get things done. Once in Phase 4: Landing, you can take a rest and focus on the spiritual portion of your journey, what we are all here for.

I can't emphasize enough the impact that Saturn has on all of our lives. There is no doubt that any individual who starts to work with this transit, not against, will be armed with one of the most important tools astrology has to offer. There have been many prominent celebrities, leaders, and presidents who have hired astrologers to assist them in planning their career according to this transit! Let's face it, JP Morgan said it best, "Millionaires don't need astrologers; billionaires do."

Start Your Exercise!
TAKING FLIGHT WITH SATURN

Saturn is the ruler of our Universe and holds great power on how your life will unfold—determine the influence Saturn currently has over the development of your life.

See sample worksheet on page 120

EXERCISE
Taking Flight with Saturn

There are four distinct phases that Saturn moves through in one cycle (29.5 years). We spend roughly 7.5 years in each phase of this cycle. These four phases correspond to the four quadrants of the Natal Chart and are labeled appropriately on this worksheet.

STEP 1:

1. When you were born, Saturn was located in one of these four quadrants/phases based on its location in the houses. In Table 1 of your Natal Chart Navigator, locate the house that Saturn was located in at the moment of your birth.

2. Using the blank inner segments of the circle, write "Natal Saturn" into the appropriate house.

STEP 2:

To determine the house Saturn currently is in, look to Table 3 of your Natal Chart Navigator. Once you determine Saturn's current location in the houses, write "Transiting Saturn" into the appropriate house of the outermost blank segment of the circle.

STEP 3:

1. We will now determine the phase Saturn was in when you were born. Look to see the quadrant and phase activated by Natal Saturn (it's written in each quadrant). Enter this phase into the first blank circle at the bottom right of the worksheet.

2. To the left bottom of the worksheet, the phases have been broken down and key words selected. Pick one key word and write it within this circle.

STEP 4:

1. We will now determine which phase Transiting Saturn activates. Determine the active phase and then enter it into the blank circle at the bottom.

2. To the left bottom of the worksheet, the phases have been broken down and key words selected. Pick one key word and write it within this circle.

* To determine your gateways, read the block entitled Navigating with Saturn—Extra!

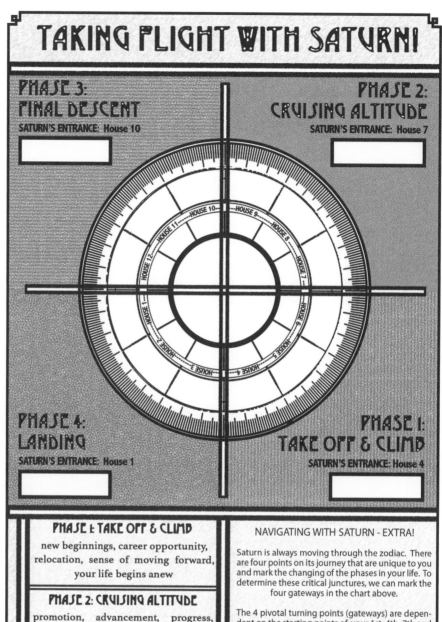

TAKING FLIGHT WITH SATURN!

PHASE 3: FINAL DESCENT
SATURN'S ENTRANCE: House 10

PHASE 2: CRUISING ALTITUDE
SATURN'S ENTRANCE: House 7

PHASE 4: LANDING
SATURN'S ENTRANCE: House 1

PHASE 1: TAKE OFF & CLIMB
SATURN'S ENTRANCE: House 4

PHASE 1: TAKE OFF & CLIMB
new beginnings, career opportunity, relocation, sense of moving forward, your life begins anew

PHASE 2: CRUISING ALTITUDE
promotion, advancement, progress, sense of covering ground, all action resulting in a culminating event

PHASE 3: FINAL DESCENT
preparation, a need to put things in order, a slight slowing down, a very purposeful time period

PHASE 4: LANDING
holding/waiting period, internal reflection, reaping the karma of past actions in this life started in phases 1 & 2

NAVIGATING WITH SATURN - EXTRA!

Saturn is always moving through the zodiac. There are four points on its journey that are unique to you and mark the changing of the phases in your life. To determine these critical junctures, we can mark the four gateways in the chart above.

The 4 pivotal turning points (gateways) are dependent on the starting points of your 1st, 4th, 7th and 10th house. Using Table 2 of your Natal Chart Navigator, you will determine the zodiac sign and degree for the pivotal House Rulers. There is a box in each quadrant where you can enter this information. Pay attention as Saturn moves through the zodiac and through the signs: Aries, Taurus, Gemini, Cancer, Leo, Virgo, Libra, Scorpio, Sagittarius, Capricorn, Aquarius and Pisces When it hits the degree notated for your specific chart and gateways, you will have begun a new phase of the Saturn transit. You can use this information to time important events and gain valuable insight into how your life will unfold. To view the current planetary positions, visit:

www.absolutelyastrology.com

I ENTERED THE SATURN CYCLE IN THE PHASE:

I'M CURRENTLY IN THIS PHASE:

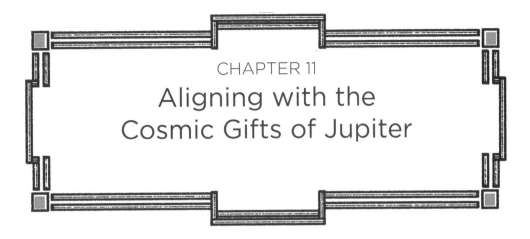

CHAPTER 11

Aligning with the Cosmic Gifts of Jupiter

POWER PLAN

△ Discover the expansive/abundant nature of Jupiter
△ Explore the impact of Jupiter through the astrological houses
△ Determine Jupiter's current location in your chart and where it's going next

Jupiter is the planet of ultimate abundance and expansion. As it transits your Natal Chart, it works its way through the houses and bestows its gifts in those particular areas of your life. It spends roughly one year in each house, completing its full cycle every 12 years. Assuming you have lived through your teenage years, you have already experienced your first natal return of Jupiter at roughly 12 years of age. This first natal return of Jupiter (when Jupiter makes one full cycle) corresponds to when adolescents enter their teenage years and begin a new cycle of growth—often associated with puberty. The second natal return of Jupiter happens at roughly twenty-four years of age, when many individuals begin the next stage of personal growth and begin to forge a life on their own.

The zodiac sign and degree that mark the starting point of each house mark the Entry Points of Jupiter (just like we explored with Saturn's Gateways). For instance, looking at Table 2 of your Natal Chart Navigator, you will see the degree and sign of each House Ruler (this is the sign and degree that begins each house). If you have 3°Scorpio ruling House 1, Jupiter enters your 1st House when it is at 3°Scorpio. As Jupiter enters each of your Houses, it activates that area of life and helps to elevate you in some way, in whichever way assists your spiritual growth at that time. This could mean you are provided with a new opportunity, perspective, or relationship. The circumstances will always be unique to your life experience and current level of development—always a perfect match to circumstance.

To illustrate the power of Jupiter, I will share with you my experience of this powerful planet in my own life. We have explored the houses throughout the previous chapters, but I would like to highlight House 5, which correlates with children, romance, and engagement. When Jupiter transits the 5th House, it is likely that you will experience one of these three things based on your specific life circumstance: children, romance, or engagement. Every Natal Chart is unique and the Entry Point for Jupiter into the 5th House will vary based on your specific birth information. In my case, the Entry Point for Jupiter into my 5th House is 2°Gemini. When Jupiter was at that location on June 21, 2012, it subsequently entered my 5th House, illuminating the opportunity for me to experience children, romance, or engagement.

When Jupiter transited this house, I was at a point in my life where I had been happily married for several years and my circumstances were such that the illumination of Jupiter through the 5th House would most likely support the expression of children. Coincidentally, I became pregnant with my son Jack in July of 2012. (Keep in mind that Jupiter began to transit on June 21, 2012.) My son was also born March 28, 2013, while Jupiter was still transiting my 5th House. I suppose that could merely be coincidence, right? But my story of the Jupiter Transit continues and even now, I'm shocked as to its complete accuracy and support in my life.

I share this information because it has been my personal validation and I hope that it helps provide you with more insight on this transit. Before I share the remainder of my story, I must first explain a slightly more advanced astrological topic. If you ever wanted to determine information on a particular area of your life, you look to the specific house in your Natal Chart that governs that area of life experience. When it comes to marriage, you look to House 7 and when it comes to children, you look to House 5. If, however, you are interested in more than the first occurrence of a child or marriage, you have to look at another house. To determine a second occurrence, you simply skip a house numerically and look to the next one. For example, the house that rules the creation of a second child is House 7 (you skip House 6); and the second occurrence of marriage is House 9 (you skip House 8). This continues to apply for third, forth, and fifth occurrences. I know this may be a little confusing, but follow along, as this is an important concept for the relevance of my story and Jupiter's influence.

Let's say for instance, you are divorced and are curious when you might enter into another union. This is more likely to occur when Jupiter transits the 9th House (second occurrence of marriage). Obviously, this is when the energy is at its strongest expression, but it in no means indicates that the

second union could only occur at that time. It simply indicates the likelihood is stronger when Jupiter transits those particular locations of your chart. This is a very important point to remember, not only in regards to the Jupiter transit, but to all astrological predictions. Astrology merely provides us with the insight to see when things are more likely to occur. It in no way indicates that events or circumstances could not occur at another time.

Having briefly explored the idea behind the second occurrence, we now have established that the 7th House rules the birth and creation of a second child. My 7th House Entry Point is 17°Cancer. My second child, Lily, was born on December 16, 2014, when Jupiter was at 18°Cancer—one degree into my 7th House. This means Jupiter was transiting my 7th House (house of the second child) when my second born, Lily, came into this world. If ever I personally needed proof of the gifts of Jupiter, I received it through the birth of my two children—in perfect harmony with this cycle. Remember, Jupiter merely highlights that area of life and lifts the likelihood of the events to occur. I have continually watched and aligned with this planet. The timing for my book being published is also in perfect alignment with the Jupiter transit—it will be transiting my 9th House when this book is released (House of Publishing).

As Jupiter moves through each house and completes its cycle, it will inevitably activate your natal planets, most importantly your Natal Sun and Natal Moon. For instance, if your Sun is located at 10°Taurus, when Jupiter is at that same degree (10°Taurus) it is activating your Natal Sun. These points where Jupiter activates the Sun or Moon are an indication that you are entering a heightened period of spiritual growth. These Power Illumination Periods vary based on your Natal Chart, but will always mark a time frame of enhanced experiences to elevate your spiritual growth.

The other indicator of a Power Illumination Period is when Jupiter transits a Power Cluster in your chart. Please don't worry about determining these periods right at this moment; we will do this in the exercise. Remember, although these gifts are freely given, we can enhance the experience by aligning our actions with Jupiter in perfect time.

When we consciously align our actions, we provide Jupiter with the support it needs to bring about the most expansion in our lives.

Jupiter, the planet of spiritual gifts, spends 12 years traveling around your chart. This means that it will spend roughly one year in each house. As it transits a house, you will often feel an energetic pull to align with its gifts in that specific area. When you complete this exercise, don't be surprised if you are actually experiencing the specific things Jupiter is illuminating. On the other hand, if you discover you aren't experiencing the gifts Jupiter could offer, do not worry. You now have all the information you need to consciously align yourself with this powerful planet. Jupiter is known for its expansive nature and for assisting individuals to live a more abundant life—it works the same for every single person.

Here is a little bit about how Jupiter supports your growth as it competes its cycle:

House 1: Activating the Inner Warrior (Cardinal Fire)

This is the House of Self-Awareness, Ego-Expression, and Physical Movement. When Jupiter is transiting this house you will find that you are entering a time of deep self-reflection. Making decisions during this time should reflect the needs of your unique spirit. This is not a time to act on another's behalf. It is important to connect with the physical body and to bridge the gap between body and spirit. This is an excellent time to start a new exercise routine or practice in your daily life. Working with movement and the breath during this time will help you access your inner wisdom and tap into its power. Jupiter is supporting you as you act "selfishly." We are of best service to the world when we have properly taken care of ourselves.

> **Top Tip:** Align with this transit by choosing to join a gym, start a new daily practice, or plan an active vacation.

House 2: Activating the Inner Builder (Fixed Earth)

This is the House of Finances, Values, and Resources. As Jupiter activates this house, you will begin to expand in one of these three areas, if not all. During this time, you will begin to discover solutions, generate ideas, and feel an overwhelming need to be more efficient with your behaviors. At times, it is easy to view our self-worth through the material possessions we obtain, but this often leads to wrong behaviors. This earth house wants you to connect with the Earth and to spend time gardening, hiking, walking your dog, and taking pleasure in the natural abundance freely given. Since this house rules not only finances, but also values, it will work hard to help assist you in becoming more abundant in a way that is congruent with positive values. This could indicate a time of financial relief in the form of a gift of money or the gift of a solution to a financial problem. If you have already been experiencing financial abundance when Jupiter transits this house, you will be called to assess how you have been managing these resources.

> **Top Tip:** Align with this transit by choosing to witness the bountiful state of nature and its natural abundance freely given—it will spark within you the deepest truth, that the spirit is infinitely abundant (and we all deserve to feel expansive).

House 3: Activating the Inner Storyteller (Mutable Air)

This is the House of Short Trips, Communication, and Learning. This is a time where Jupiter is supporting exploration and stepping out from the norm. This could be an excellent time to learn a foreign language (it rules verbal communication) or to sign up for a class to learn something new. There will be an overwhelming amount of mental energy during this time—you will now be able to focus into a particular pursuit or multiple pursuits that inspire you. Since this House rules communication, it is likely you will reconnect with old friends, receive a phone call from someone you lost touch with, or even find yourself bumping into people you know when out running errands. We grow tremendously in this life through our relationships and dialogues, and Jupiter reminds us of this.

> **Top Tip:** Align with this transit by choosing to explore something new—take advantage of the extra mental energy you will experience during this time period.

House 4: Activating the Inner Nurturer (Cardinal Water)

This is the House of Private, Personal, Family, and Home. During Jupiter's transit through this house, you will feel a need to set down roots and establish a strong foundation in your life. This energy can express in a multitude of ways depending on your life circumstances, but it always centers around the home. You may find this is a time you are purchasing your first home, moving into a new home, or renovating the home you have. This desire stems from this house activating your Inner Nurturer and your natural desire to care not only for yourself, but others. The expression of this energy will support you actively creating your chosen family. You want to feel loved and safe during this time, using your immediate environment to help support those emotions. Jupiter will help make this possible for you in your life. It is preparing you now to take a turn to this new quadrant in the chart and paving a way for you to receive the gifts that are on the way.

> **Top Tip:** Align with this transit by choosing to set down roots and move into a new stage of your life. You may benefit from organizing, rearranging, or renovating your home—you may also find that you will purchase and move to a new home during this transit.

House 5: Activating the Inner Performer (Fixed Fire)

This is the House of Creative Expression, Romance, and Children. This house is about creation and bringing something new into this world. This can express in a multitude of ways, but one thing always remains consistent—you are bringing something new into your life that was not there before. Depending on your specific life circumstances, this could be a new romance, engagement, birth of a child, or new creative expression or invention. The activation of the inner Performer assists you in feeling empowered and pushes you to believe in your dreams during this time. This means you are more likely to act on a desire or take a chance you wouldn't normally take. You may feel "lucky" and be willing to explore life in ways you hadn't before, but ensure that this is in alignment with your deeper desires for your life. For instance, you may get the urge to go out and gamble (and might just win during this time), but the true calling of this transit is to work towards your personal dream and life ambition.

> **Top Tip:** Align with this transit by choosing to create in any way that feels inspirational to you. Harness the child-like spirit and perspective—jump, even if you don't know where you'll land.

House 6: Activating the Inner Craftsman (Mutable Earth)

This is the House of Daily Habits, Physical Health, and Work Environment. During this time you will begin to re-assess how you spend your time and the habits you've created over the years. You might find yourself pondering some new questions, "Do I enjoy my job and co-workers?" "Am I physically feeling my best?" and "What do I truly want to do with my time?" This natural urge will assist you in making changes to your life, which perhaps you had been avoiding up until this point. This can express as a new exercise routine, healthier diet, or even the purchase of new furry friend (nothing like a pet to change up your daily routine!). Since this house rules habits, it is also an appropriate time for breaking habits as well. You may feel called (or be forced) to quit smoking, drinking, or gambling during this time. The idea is that your daily activities will be changing and definitely for the better.

> **Top Tip:** Align with this transit by choosing to actively assess your life circumstance. If you're unsatisfied with any portion of your life, take action to move yourself forward (Jupiter will provide a more favorable outcome if you do).

House 7: Activating the Inner Peacemaker (Cardinal Air)

This is the House of Partnerships, Relationships, and Contracts. As Jupiter transits this house, it has one specific goal: to help you attract and maintain relationships that are serving your highest good. This transit will heighten all happenings that you experience through romantic partnership, friendships, co-workers, etc. Since Jupiter is an amplifier in this house, you will see your circumstances expanded upon. If you were or are in a healthy, loving relationship, this will mark the time for a deeper connection or for rekindling of that flame. If you are single, you will most likely receive more opportunities for dating and finding an appropriate mate. If, however, you are in an unhealthy and destructive relationship, Jupiter will create the circumstances to help you get rid of that relationship once and for all. Trust that Jupiter is acting on behalf of your highest self and has one goal: to bring you relationships that serve your highest good.

> **Top Tip:** Align with this transit by choosing to pay attention to the development of relationships—trust that Jupiter knows what it is doing for you (if a relationship leaves you during this time, know that it was for the highest good of all).

House 8: Activating the Inner Alchemist (Fixed Water)

This is the House of Spiritual Transformation, Heightened Intuition, Legal Concerns, and Other People's Money. This is a time where you will inevitably find yourself asking the bigger questions: What is my purpose? Am I really a spirit? What happens after I die? Jupiter is here to assist you in understanding the function of life on the physical plane. You will be provided with opportunities to deepen your connection to spirit during this time—in a way that is most comfortable to you at your current spiritual state. This house also indicates that money may be making its way to you down different channels and not from your current job. This could indicate an inheritance, spouse receiving a promotion, winning lottery ticket, or simply a gift. Use this time to strengthen the connection between mind, body, and spirit. * Legal concerns are of heightened importance during this time.

> **Top Tip:** Align with this transit by choosing to explore deeper truths in any way that inspires you—occult studies, writing, meditation, etc. There is a heightened connection between spirit and body during this time.

House 9: Activating the Inner Philosopher (Mutable Fire)

This is the House of Travel, Education, Literature, and Publishing. Jupiter assists you here as you tap into your more philosophical side and begin to approach the world with new vigor. That deeper life purpose you discovered in House 8 is now being called to life! This is a time of mental pursuits and you may soon find you are reading book after book with an insatiable hunger for knowledge. This new hunger lends itself well to foreign travel and new journeys. You may finally be ready to go on that exotic adventure, for the conditions will now be in your favor. Ruling higher education, this is an excellent time to apply and enroll in school. If you have been putting it off for financial reasons, that scholarship you were searching for is more likely to appear during this time. If you are a writer, this is the time to get published (this house rules the written word). Things are definitely coming together for you at this time and new opportunity awaits!

> **Top Tip:** Align with this transit by choosing to pursue something that is intellectually and spiritually challenging—this is a time to expand beyond measure.

House 10: Activating the Inner Entrepreneur (Cardinal Earth)

This is the House of Career, Calling, and Social Activities. This is a time to get noticed in the public and you will find that you're in the spotlight (in one way or another). You are being called to center stage and will have an opportunity to shine! Jupiter assists you in tapping into your highest potential here and wants you to lead by example. If you are doing public speaking of any kind, you will be at your best as Jupiter transits this house. If you are an actor, you might land your first leading role. There is some sort of career shift that typically takes place during this time that promises you bigger rewards. Think promotion, new career opportunity, or a long-awaited "big break."

> **Top Tip:** Align with this transit by choosing to follow your deeper purpose for this life during this time. Events, circumstances, and people will show up to illuminate the way.

House 11: Activating the Inner Inventor (Fixed Air)

This is the House of Invention, Humanitarian Work, and Your Chosen People. Jupiter is supporting you as you assess the people you choose to surround yourself with in this life. Each person emanates a vibrational field; are you surrounding yourself with people at the top of your potential, helping to push you forward? Or are you choosing to connect with those at the lower end of your field, keeping you from accessing your next steps? You are being called to give back, and Jupiter is asking you to put out into the world that which you are seeking. This house is all about moving society to the next level (technologically or spiritually) in some way and working for the collective good. This is a perfect time for charity work and giving back in any way that you can. This could be helping a friend in need or donating a small or large sum of money to a charity. It is about doing what you can and thinking outside the box.

> **Top Tip:** Align with this transit by choosing to give back in any way that you can: volunteer, donate, and get involved. Everything you give out to the world always returns to you (sometimes down different channels).

House 12: Activating the Inner Artist (Mutable Water)

This is the House of Spirit, Faith, and Dreams. This house is a culminating house pulling everything together. This is a perfect time to take up a new spiritual practice or to commit to one you lost along the way. You may be very reflective during this time. This house rules dreams and you may begin to receive messages from the other side through this medium. It is a time for deep connection with others and emotional art. You are drawn now to film and exploring the emotional journey of others. You are left

wondering, "Have I used the gifts that were given to me?" and, "Have I taken the time to self-nurture and give back?" This is how Jupiter prepares you for another 12-year journey through the houses.

> **Top Tip:** Align with this transit by choosing to surround yourself with whatever creative expression speaks to you.

Wow. If you're like me, you are already gathering speed and are ready to see if this energy can work for you in your life. Jupiter is all about timing and you have the opportunity to claim your power and align with the gifts it can bring.

On my honeymoon, my husband and I were inspired to grab boogie boards and play in the sun. There I would spend the afternoon, floating and trying to catch the waves. Sometimes the waves would only nudge me forward a little ways. But sometimes, if I caught the wave just right, I flew effortlessly. Propelling myself with ease to the sand. Weightless. And there I would be lying in the sunshine, staring back at the ocean and at the waves that had already receded. Sometimes when we do things at just the right time, we can soar further and accomplish more—why not consciously choose to align with this power? Why not consciously choose to align with the magical gifts of Jupiter?

Start Your Exercises!
ALIGNING WITH THE COSMIC GIFTS OF JUPITER
EXTRA—KEEPING TRACK OF JUPITER

At certain times in our life we are able to soak up the cosmic rays like a sponge. Here we explore transiting Jupiter as it shifts our spiritual focus roughly every year in a 12-year cycle.

See sample worksheet on page 121

EXERCISE
Aligning with the Cosmic Gifts of Jupiter

STEP 1:

Before exploring the impact of Transiting Jupiter, we first must determine our Power Illumination Periods. We do this by entering our Natal Sun, Natal Moon, and relevant Power Clusters on to the worksheet. Looking to Table 1 of your Natal Chart Navigator, determine the house location for your Natal Sun and Natal Moon. Enter their location into the outermost blank portion of the Natal Chart circle.

STEP 2:

We originally explored Power Clusters (3 or more planets in a house) in chapter 1. Looking back to the second exercise for that chapter, determine if you identified a Power Cluster in your chart. If one was present, add "Power Cluster" to the outermost circle and appropriate house.

STEP 3:

Using Table 3 of your Natal Chart Navigator, determine the house that Jupiter is currently transiting in your chart. Once this is determined, shade in the innermost blank segment of the Natal Chart that corresponds to that house. Remember, if you shaded a house that also has the Sun, Moon, or Power Cluster, you are currently in a Power Illumination Period.

STEP 4:

1. In this chapter there is a detailed description of Jupiter's impact in each house. Looking back in the chapter, locate the house that Jupiter is currently transiting in your chart.

2. Based on your reflection of this information, write a sentence on its impact next to "Current Impact" (at the top of the worksheet beneath the title). Note, if Jupiter is transiting a house of a Power Illumination Period, add "Power Illumination Period."

STEP 5:

1. It's time to determine what Jupiter has in store for you next! Jupiter moves through the houses numerically: if it is currently in House 9, it will be moving to House 10 next. Look back in the chapter to read more about the house Jupiter will transit next.

2. Write one sentence next to the "Coming Up" section (at the top of this exercise). Note, if Jupiter will be transiting a house of a Power Illumination Period, add "Power Illumination Period."

CURRENT IMPACT: COMING UP:

HOUSE 1   ENTRY POINT:
HOUSE 2   ENTRY POINT:
HOUSE 3   ENTRY POINT:
HOUSE 4   ENTRY POINT:
HOUSE 5   ENTRY POINT:
HOUSE 6   ENTRY POINT:
HOUSE 7   ENTRY POINT:
HOUSE 8   ENTRY POINT:
HOUSE 9   ENTRY POINT:
HOUSE 10   ENTRY POINT:
HOUSE 11   ENTRY POINT:
HOUSE 12   ENTRY POINT:

EXTRA—KEEPING TRACK OF JUPITER

You can easily align with the gifts of Jupiter by watching it journey through your chart! To determine when Jupiter will enter a new house, we will add the house Entry Points into the boxes above. Looking to Table 2 of your Natal Chart Navigator, enter the sign and degree of your House Ruler into the squares. When Jupiter is at those specific degrees, it is entering a new house in your chart and illuminating that area of your life.

You can keep track of the current location of Jupiter at www.absolutelyastrology.com.

In this exercise, you determined the location of your Sun, Moon, and Power Clusters. This information indicates a Power Illumination Period. Add "Power Illumination Period" into the squares to keep track of when Jupiter will enter those periods! Time your actions for heightened results!

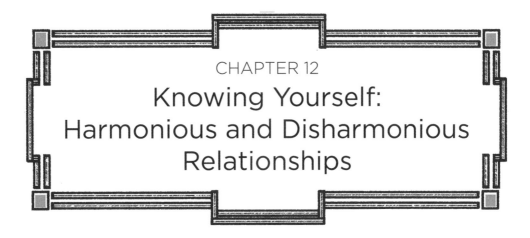

CHAPTER 12
Knowing Yourself: Harmonious and Disharmonious Relationships

POWER PLAN

△ Understand why relationships are either harmonious, disharmonious, or neutral
△ Discover the General Significant Relationship Indicator approach to Synastry
△ Learn about the four Heightened Indicators through aspects: Conjunction, Trine, Opposition, and Square

The exciting thing about this new area we are moving into is that we can take the precise location of your Rising Sign in comparison to that of another's and voila! We are able to determine the nature of that relationship. This process by which we compare your Natal Chart information to another's is called Synastry. By looking at the angular relationships between planets/sensitive points, we will begin to understand the inherent dynamic present in every relationship: from co-worker to lover, from parent to child. Understanding how the planets/sensitive points interact with one another and potentially form aspects (angles), allows us to uncover the mystery behind why certain relationships function the way that they do.

We all know the saying, "Location! Location! Location!" So it should come as no surprise that the location of your planets at birth, in relation to another's, is a very powerful predictor as to how that relationship will function. If you've been validated by the information you have discovered

so far about yourself, you will be blown away by what you learn in this chapter. This part is looking at how the signs (element and mode) will interact with one another. One very powerful approach to Synastry is to compare Rising Signs/Ascendants because these signs express how an individual will approach life. When we interact with others who naturally approach life in a similar fashion—we will naturally become more harmonious.

I know this example may come across as a little too obvious, but it is a very easy way to think about this concept. We have all played with magnets at some point in our lives. As you move two magnets together, you can literally feel the reaction even before they physically touch each other. You can feel the magnets pushing for that connection—as they approach one another, the impulse becomes stronger and the process becomes smooth, easy, and reliable. On the other hand—you can feel when the magnets aren't a correct match and they push each other away. We are all, in many ways, human magnets—we each are a bundle of energy and we either repel or attract. In astrological terms, we are either: harmonious, disharmonious, or neutral with other beings we interact with.

Before proceeding, I recommend going back to chapter 1—A Glimpse at Astrology (on page 14), and re-reading the descriptions of each element: fire, earth, air, and water, along with the descriptions of each mode: cardinal, fixed, and mutable. This way you can ensure you follow the concepts within this chapter as easily as possible. It is through these very approaches to life (the 12 signs broken down to element and mode) that we will determine the harmonious and disharmonious indicators that can occur between two people. The table that follows lists the element and mode for each sign.

The Element and Mode of the Twelve Signs of the Zodiac:

SIGN	ELEMENT	MODE
Aries	Fire	Cardinal
Taurus	Earth	Fixed
Gemini	Air	Mutable
Cancer	Water	Cardinal
Leo	Fire	Fixed
Virgo	Earth	Mutable
Libra	Air	Cardinal
Scorpio	Water	Fixed
Sagittarius	Fire	Mutable
Capricorn	Earth	Cardinal
Aquarius	Air	Fixed
Pisces	Water	Mutable

This technique of Synastry (the comparison of two charts) allows us to use the Ascendant/Rising Sign to predict how a relationship will function over the long-term. Because this is an advanced topic—I will be repetitive to ensure that you understand the concept (sorry to those who may already be familiar with this technique). The first step is to take a broad approach—looking first to the actual sign of the Ascendant (Rising Sign). By looking at the specific signs, we learn a lot rather quickly and with much ease.

Please note, the Ascendant is not the Sun Sign and thus, you may have to do a little digging to uncover the individual's Ascendant/Rising Sign (best not to ask on the first date!). In order for the Rising Sign to be calculated correctly there must be an accurate birth time.

It's very important to first start by assessing the General Significant Relationship Indicator (GSRI), which is done through element and mode (sign). General Significant Relationship Indicators (GSRI) can be either harmonious or disharmonious. Really, the GSRI works as a way to pick up broad patterns and gives us a quick and easy way to determine how two people will interact. Once the GSRI is determined (and only if this is determined), then we look to see if there is an additional Heightened Indicator for that specific relationship (an aspect).

Heightened Indicators are only strengthening the information that was discovered originally by the GSRI. That means that if you don't over-think things too much, this is an easy way to determine how a relationship will function.

Essentially, we start by just comparing the signs and deciding if a GSRI has been made. Then we look to see if a Heightened Indicator is formed (this is done by determining if an aspect was formed). Make sense? I hope so, but if not—the exercise is designed to help you determine all of the concepts you learn in this chapter.

Your Rising Sign is the combination of an element: fire, earth, air, water, and a mode: cardinal, fixed, and mutable. For instance, Taurus Rising is Fixed Earth, and Sagittarius Rising is Mutable Fire. Based on the combination of the element and mode that make the Rising Sign, we are able to predict the most probable outcome for how a relationship will function.

This is a very insightful tool and I recommend exploring relationships with parents, children, friends, lovers, enemies (if you can get their information), and anyone else who sparks your interest. Obviously, you will need their Rising Sign to use this technique, but you can also look at the Sun and Moon (which we will discuss briefly in a bit).

Remember, this is all about probable outcomes—it is not a full guarantee. I have personally found this technique to be very accurate, but that isn't to say there is only ever one possible outcome (we know this isn't true because we live in a world of fate and free will). What I appreciate the most about Synastry is the lessons it teaches. It has shed much light on situations, relationships, and dynamics I have experienced throughout my life, I hope it does for you as well.

Rising Signs that are in the same element will always have gifts to share with each other: fire with fire, earth with earth, air with air, and water with water. This is because the element represents a specific approach to life; when two individuals' approach to life is similar, they most certainly will experience a level of harmony within their relationship. If you discover that you have your Rising Sign in the fire element and your child's is as well, you are essentially "cut from the same cloth" so to speak. When you interact with someone whose Rising Sign is in the same element, you will naturally feel deeply validated, safe, and understood. Through the kindred approach to life, you will have similar behavioral and emotional tendencies, which make it much easier for you to interact over the long-term.

Rising Signs in the same element are a GSRI that we talked about earlier (General Significant Relationship Indicator). In this case, it is a Harmonious GSRI because of element. Since we determined the GSRI through element, we would now look to see if there was an additional Heightened Indicator by aspect. An aspect occurs when the planets/points have a specific degree in between them. This acts as another marker, indicating the strength and potential of the relationship. In the case where the element is the same, there are only two significant aspects that could have been made: either the Conjunction (0-degrees apart) or the Trine (120-degrees apart).

The trine and conjunction are two harmonious aspects, but with differing effects. The trine is complementary in nature since it brings two different modes together with the same element. Rising Signs that trine one another (4°Taurus Rising with 4°Virgo Rising, for example) work together, sharing their unique strengths to propel each other towards their goals. On the other hand, when they are in the same sign (4°Taurus Rising with 4°Taurus Rising), a conjunction has been formed, and they are thus in the same element and mode. This constitutes a very powerful blending of the energies together into one singular focus. This is a true melding and can oftentimes be felt more intensely because of how much their spirits resonate with one another.

To check for an aspect, we have to compare the degrees of the Rising Signs to see if they meet the criteria. As I mentioned earlier, the trine is when planets/points are 120-degrees apart and the conjunction occurs when they are 0-degrees apart. As planets approach this distance, the harmonics begin to intensify (just like when you feel the pull or repel of a magnet). This means that the aspect does not have to be exact to be considered significant—it just needs to be approaching exact. Astrologers use what is termed an "orb," which allows the aspect to be labeled significant if it is within a certain degree of the exact aspect. The traditional orb used is 7-degrees.

We're going to break it down a little bit here, just to make sure you understand why this concept works. Each element trines (120-degrees apart) one another in the zodiac. 1°Taurus is 120 degrees from 1°Virgo, which is 120 degree from 1°Capricorn, which is 120 degrees from 1°Taurus. This is true of each element and is symbolic of the harmonious nature between the signs, and specifically the element. An aspect between two points can be calculated by determining the degrees between one another—the stronger the aspect is to exact, the more powerful the indication of harmony. Remember, if it is within the 7-degree orb, it is significant.

Each sign is 30°, so keep this in mind as we dive deeper in to determine if an aspect has been formed. In the case of the trine (120 degrees apart), we would consider it a trine when it is within 113°–127° apart (adding and subtracting 7-degrees to the perfect trine of 120-degrees). Keep in mind that planets/sensitive points can be 120 degrees apart, but if they do not meet the GSRI through element, this is a dissociative aspect and not to be considered with our particular approach. 29°Taurus Rising matched to 1°Libra Rising, although technically almost a perfect trine, is not a GSRI for our purposes because the elements are different—Taurus is Earth, Libra is Air.

Now that you understand a little bit more about identifying aspects and why they are important, I will teach you the shortcut. All you need to know is the degree of your Rising Sign, then both add and subtract 7 to determine your orb. For instance, if you have 15°Taurus, then your orb would be 8°–22°. Any person who has their Rising Sign in the same element (earth in this case), within 8°–22°, is in aspect to you. This means a Heightened Indicator is present. The question you should be asking at that point, "Is it the trine aspect or the conjunction aspect?"

If the Rising Sign are in different signs (Taurus Rising with Virgo Rising/Capricorn Rising) then a trine was formed, assuming the degree falls within your orb. Once again, using that example above, 15°Taurus with 18°Virgo is in trine (both a GSRI and a Heightened Indicator). This would be the most harmonious relationship indication that you can find. The trine is expansive, positive, and in flow with the energetic forces of the unseen. It feels easy to be in a relationship with someone when the Rising Signs are in trine. This is because, just like magnets, once that orb has been entered, it is inevitably going to be very easy to connect, again and again.

Don't worry if at times you feel slightly overwhelmed by this new information. This is an extra advanced concept that will enhance the basics if you choose to delve further in—now or at a later time. Your goal now is to absorb the information as best as you can. Just envision yourself as a magnet; know that there will be some energies that harmonize and are attracted together, where others will repel. Once you complete this chapter's exercise, you will have created a Compatibility Report that lists out all the harmonious and disharmonious indicators for your specific Rising Sign.

If their Rising Sign is in the exact same sign (Taurus Rising/Taurus Rising), a conjunction has been formed, assuming their degree falls within your orb. Remember, the conjunction is 0 degrees apart. Using the example above, 15°Taurus Rising with 8°Taurus Rising is in conjunction (both a GSRI and a Heightened Indicator are present). Think about that magnet—they have entered that distance where the repel or attract mechanism will come into play. In this case, it is attracting the other person, although as you will soon find out—the repel function exists as well.

We have all experienced a harmonic relationship in our lives. If you've ever met someone and immediately clicked or saw eye-to-eye, there was most certainly a harmonic interplay between your Natal Charts through the Rising Sign or other significant planets, like the Sun or Moon. But how about when you meet someone and they just seemed to immediately rub you the wrong way? Or when you thought you saw eye-to-eye, but came to find out that they were not who you thought they were? In those two last cases, the opposite GSRI has been formed and it is of a disharmonious nature.

Harmonic relationships occur because of the element and disharmonic relationships occur because of the mode. The disharmonious aspects are the Square (90-degrees apart) and the Opposition (180-degrees apart). These aspects always have the same mode: cardinal, fixed, or mutable, but with different elements. Each mode has four signs: Cardinal (Aries, Cancer, Libra, Capricorn), Fixed (Taurus, Leo, Scorpio, Aquarius), and Mutable (Gemini, Virgo, Sagittarius, Pisces).

The opposition is easy to comprehend because these are the signs that appear opposite one another in the zodiac. Aries opposes Libra, Taurus opposes Scorpio, Gemini opposes Sagittarius, Cancer opposes Capricorn, Leo opposes Aquarius, and Virgo opposes Pisces.

There is something very curious about the opposition because, in all cases, they are in the same mode, with complementary elements. Of the four elements, each has a complementary pair. Earth and water elements are complementary, as are fire and air elements.

Earth is practical and hard working and appreciates the heart and warmth of water. Water loves the consistent and predictable nature of earth and feels very safe under those circumstances. Air is very intellectual and craves stimulating conversation, which jives very well with action-oriented fire. Fire loves to cause change and air loves to think about causing change. These complementary elements work well together, but because the modes are the same, they will eventually clash under most circumstances. Note: complementary elements where the modes are not the same react quite differently with one another—they have the potential to interact positively over the long-term. This is a concept we dive deeply into in the free workshop on the 4 Elements of Spirit. It allows you to see another layer to the magnetic relationship that can occur between two people. If you want to explore this deeper layer to relationships, you can sign up for this free workshop at www.absolutelyastrology.com/freeworkshop.

In the case of the opposing Rising Signs (when element is complementary and mode is the same) a specific type of GSRI has been made. This is where you thought you would get along swimmingly (complementary elements), but then find yourselves almost always butting heads (ironically because you have the same mode active). Rising Signs that oppose each other will discover that they do typically have one very important thing in common, but then for some reason, they don't click beyond that. This is because they are naturally set up to oppose each other—a natural push and pull typically occurs!

For example, Cancer (cardinal water) opposes Capricorn (cardinal earth). These complementary elements will always both strive to bring people together and to enable a group of individuals to form a tight and efficient bond. The trouble comes in to play with how they go about reaching that end goal. Capricorn will most likely use its cardinal urge to lay down the law and create order for the benefit of all. On the other hand, Cancer uses its cardinal urge to connect and lead from an emotional place—often viewing Capricorn's rules as "harsh limitations" when they don't align with their own feelings. The tug of war is always happening in the opposition. If there is a Heightened Indicator, it will be a push and pull that you feel constantly—just like when the magnets approach that barrier where they begin to push each other away. Ironically, this very aspect creates the dynamic, passionate love affair—it burns brightly at first, and then disintegrates until nothing is left.

The other Heightened Indicator is the square aspect (90-degrees apart). Each sign in the zodiac has two signs that square them. Just as you might have guessed, now we are looking at signs with the same mode, but with uncomplementary elements. Fire and air are both uncomplementary to the other two elements: earth and water. Obviously this means that earth and water are then uncomplementary to fire and air. This is the most frustrating aspect and a particularly challenging relationship to be in. Here the action-oriented behaviors of both individuals are the same (cardinal, fixed, or mutable), but they go about it in totally different ways that do not blend—like oil and water. Fire and air do not easily blend with earth (too practical) or water (too emotional). Earth and water do not easily blend with fire (too aggressive) or air (too detached). This inherent struggle to see eye-to-eye is the root of why these energies typically do not get along in a harmonious way.

The square is something we have all experienced and won't soon forget. You could probably name a few people just off the top of your head that you never could see eye-to-eye with. The key understanding here is that different approaches to life may or may not jive well with one another, but this does not in any way mean that one is superior to the next. Just because you approach something head on does not mean it is a better way to live than another's. These are merely different approaches being expressed on the physical plane—and each approach is valid for that specific individual.

If a GSRI is formed by the same mode being present, this indicates that it will be a relationship that will require give and take. If you further discover a Heightened Indicator by the square or opposition, sparks will fly and fights may happen. Just as we discovered that the trine and conjunction occur based on the specific distance in between, the same is true for the square and opposition. The square occurs when there is a distance of 90 degrees and the opposition occurs when the distance is 180 degrees. We once again use a 7-degree orb because like the magnet, the effects become apparent as the aspect approaches being exact.

Where the opposition has some pros (due to the complementary element), the square Heightened Indicator does not. With the Heightened Indicator of the square, there won't be much common ground. Just like magnets that naturally repel each other, you can't get them to stick. In these relationships, the individuals (with conscious effort) would have to find other ways to harmonize (perhaps through other commonalities in their charts). The most powerful thing to do in these situations is to reach deep within yourself and honor that although your approach may differ from theirs, both are equal and valid.

Please note, I'm not saying that the disharmonious relationships are terrible and there is no point to being in them—I'm just saying they will take work. Maybe that is something that you need (and let's face it, we all do at some points in our lives) to learn, grow, and expand. There will always be many lessons to learn from the relationships that form the square or opposition. However, having them in the form of a marriage versus a friendship makes a difference.

It is unavoidable that you will have to interact with someone whose Rising Sign squares or opposes your own at some point in this life, but if you can avoid marrying or going into a business partnership with this energy dynamic, all the better for you. Like I said—these relationships are work and require effort. It's one thing

to consciously choose a friendship with this dynamic and quite another thing to marry, go into business with, or form a legal contract with this dynamic.

In this exercise, you will determine the GSRI and Heightened Indicators for your Rising Sign. This is a powerful tool that must be used with a deep respect for the unseen energetic forces within us all. While I would urge you to do what you can and to make conscious harmonizing choices, there are times when this is not possible. There is a chance that you are the child, parent, or sibling to someone who may form a disharmonious aspect to your Rising Sign. Remember, those types of relationships were often fated and charted before you incarnated (you chose it!). It is very important that you honor the decisions you made on the other side and dig within yourself to understand why you chose that type of relationship in the first place. When it comes to the fated relationships: mother, father, sibling, or child, it is not right to abandon or walk away because things are disharmoniously aspected and you don't see eye-to-eye. There is most certainly a gift and karmic unfolding active (although hidden) within a fated relationship that promises great expansion for you in this life.

If there is no GSRI present (this means no Heightened Indicator as well), it is a neutral relationship based on the Rising Signs. There may be dynamics between the Sun and Moon, but we must take these things one step at a time and for now, we are using the Rising Signs to learn about the dynamics in a relationship. This brings me to my last point: there is one other very important piece to consider when it comes to predicting the dynamics of a relationship, the harmony between the Sun and Moon. If their Moon is in the same sign as your Sun, or their Sun is in the same sign as your Moon, there will most likely be harmony because a deeper connection has been made on the internal level. It is always good practice to look at the location of the Sun and Moon because even in the case of a square between Rising Signs, sometimes a more complex relationship can be formed through a different type of harmony.

Although it is vitally important to find those who harmonize with us in this life, we should never judge or be hurtful to those who do not. When choice is involved, choose wisely. Where fate sets in, act accordingly. Always claim your power by choosing harmonious relationships whenever you can, but also seek to claim your power by choosing harmony where it does not naturally thrive—for in some cases, we may have no choice.

What Now?

For relationships you are currently in, you have been given a gift that must be used for its highest purpose. Use this information to align yourself with individuals who complement and validate your being. Chances are, you already know which relationships are disharmonious and which ones are harmonious. If you are able to obtain

the birth information of another to compare Ascendants, use this information wisely and for validation purposes. Oil and water do mix for very brief times, but this requires effort and constant supervision. They will always separate without constant effort and attention. Based on the astrological aspects, you will know the nature behind your relationships. The only question you need to ask yourself is, "Is this what I am currently seeking?"

HANDY TIP

Ready to embrace this new insight? You can easily cut the Compatibility Report out of this book and use it for reference. If you're entering into a new partnership with someone you have not known for very long, a quick look at the relationship between your Ascendants is priceless.

Start Your Exercises!
COMPATIBILITY REPORT

Astrology has a powerful way of revealing fundamental truths and wisdom rather quickly—use this gift to explore the hidden dynamics within your relationships.

See sample worksheet on pages 122–123

COMPATIBILITY REPORT:

I am most compatible with another when their Rising Sign/Ascendant is in the same Element as my own.

The element of my Rising Sign is:

_____

The three signs of this element are:

1.

2.

3.

To determine if there is an additional harmonic indication, we can look to see if an aspect has been formed. When Rising Sign's are in the same element, there are only two aspects that can be formed: the trine (120-degrees apart) and the conjunction (0-degrees apart). Follow instructions in Exercise - Part 1, enter your allowable orb here:

_____ -- _____

 My sun is in the sign:

....if their Moon is in this same sign, this is a strong indication of harmony.

My Moon is in the sign:

....if their Sun is in this same sign, this is a strong indication of harmony.

Without other harmonious indications, those whose Ascendant squares or oppose my Ascendant, will most likely result in a disharmonious relationship. These three signs are:

1.

2.

3.

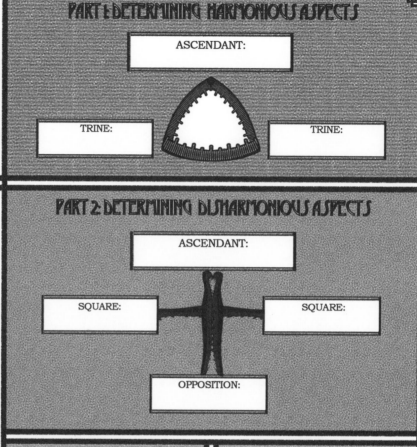

HARMONIOUS ASPECTS

TRINE: HARMONIOUS ASPECT
(120-degrees apart)
Harmonious relationship due to the activation of the same element. Below lists the signs that trine each other.

FIRE:

Aries   Leo   Sagittarius

EARTH:

Taurus   Virgo   Capricorn

AIR:

Gemini   Libra   Aquarius

WATER:

Cancer   Scorpio   Pisces

CONJUNCTION: HARMONIOUS ASPECT
(0-degrees apart)
Harmonious relationship due to the activation of the same Element and Mode. This means that they are in the exact same sign. If they are within 7-degrees of each other, then the aspect is heightened.

DISHARMONIOUS ASPECTS

OPPOSITION: DISHARMONIOUS ASPECT
(180-degrees apart)
Signs that appear across from one another in the zodiac are in opposition.

Aries - Libra
Taurus - Scorpio
Gemini - Sagittarius
Cancer - Capricorn
Leo - Aquarius
Virgo - Pisces

SQUARE: DISHARMONIOUS ASPECT
(90-degrees apart)
Disharmonious relationship due to the activation of the same mode, but being in different elements. Below lists each sign and the two signs that square it.

Aries: Cancer & Capricorn
Taurus: Leo & Aquarius
Gemini: Virgo & Pisces
Cancer: Libra & Aries
Leo: Scorpio & Taurus
Virgo: Sagittarius & Gemini
Libra: Capricorn & Cancer
Scorpio: Aquarius & Leo
Sagittarius: Pisces & Virgo
Capricorn: Aries & Libra
Aquarius: Taurus & Scorpio
Pisces: Gemini & Sagittarius

EXERCISE
Relationship Compatibility through the Aspects

There are four primary aspects that can be made between planets/sensitive points. Two are considered harmonious: the trine and the conjunction. Two are considered disharmonious: the square and the opposition. When looking to see how you will interact with a companion, business partner, employee, or friend, you can compare your charts to determine how harmonious or disharmonious the union may be. Please note, disharmonious aspects are not necessarily an indication that you should immediately abandon the relationship. They merely indicate that there will be more "kinks" to work out along the way.

PART 1—DIRECTIONS

STEP 1:
The strongest indicator for whether or not a relationship will be harmonious can be determined by comparing the position of the Ascendant/Rising Sign. Just as certain musical notes blend well, others do not. Your Rising Sign will interact with each of the 12 signs in specific ways. Because of this ability to determine if planets will harmonize or not, Astrology can be utilized to predict how two individuals would most likely function in a relationship.

Use the information in Table 1 of your Natal Chart Navigator to enter the sign and degree of your Ascendant into the worksheet Part 1.

* Remember the Ascendant/Rising Sign are being compared, not the Sun Signs.

STEP 2:
Rising Signs that share the same element will naturally be more compatible with one another. This is because they approach life in a similar fashion, and they will naturally harmonize through their behaviors, goals, and values. In the Harmonious Aspects Key in the shaded lower left middle section of the worksheet, the signs have been sorted by element for you.

1. When you locate your sign and element, add the remaining two signs into the worksheet, Part 1.

2. Go ahead and enter the element of your Rising Sign and the three signs you recorded into the Compatibility Report.

STEP 3:
This harmonious indication (determined when elements are the same) can be heightened. If the Rising Signs are in aspect to one another, this serves as further validation to the harmonic indication. There are only two aspects that can be formed when in the same element: the Conjunction (0-degrees apart) and the Trine (120-degrees apart). Remember, the aspect does not need to be exact to be significant. This is why we need to determine what the allowable orb is for your chart.

1. Look to the worksheet in Part 1 to see the degree you entered for your Rising Sign, then both add and subtract 7-degrees from this number to determine the allowable orb.

2. Please add this information to the Compatibility Report.

* Note, if the Rising Sign of another is in this allowable orb, an aspect has been made. If it is in the same sign, a conjunction is formed. If it is one of the other two signs, a trine has been formed.

STEP 4:
The other strong indication of a harmonious relationship occurs if your Sun is located in the same sign as their Moon or if your Moon is located in the same sign as their Sun. Using Table 1 in your Natal Chart Navigator, add this information to the Compatibility Report accordingly.

*Note: If the Moons are in the same sign, this is also a harmonious indication.

PART 2—DIRECTIONS

STEP 1:
There are three Rising Signs that you will naturally struggle to harmonize with. These three signs consist of the two signs that Square your Ascendant/Rising Sign and the sign that opposes it.

To determine the disharmonious signs, enter your Ascendant/Rising Sign and degree into the worksheet, Part 2.

STEP 2:
To determine the sign that opposes your Ascendant, look to the lower portion of the Disharmonious Aspects Key in the shaded area at the lower middle left on the worksheet: there will be six pairs of signs that are in opposition. When you locate your sign within one of these pairs, the other sign that it is paired with represents the sign that it opposes. Enter this sign into the box for "Opposition" in the worksheet, Part 2. This sign is naturally 180 degrees apart from your Rising Sign and appears on the opposite side of the zodiac.

* Note, this is a particularly curious combination and can often indicate a relationship that comes on strong, but does not withstand the test of time. This is due to the complementary element and same mode as discussed in the chapter.

STEP 3:
The next step is to determine the two signs that square your Ascendant. In the upper portion of the Disharmonious Aspect Key, there is a list of all 12 signs and the two signs that square them. Locate the sign of your Ascendant/Rising Sign and then enter the two signs into the boxes in the worksheet, Part 2. If an individual has their Ascendant in one of these two signs, the relationship will most likely be disharmonious. Just like oil separates from water, there are some combinations of energies that simply do not harmonize well. This is not to the fault of any one type of individual, but rather to the inherent nature involved with the differing approaches, tendencies, and traits we bring into each incarnation.

STEP 4:
Enter these three signs into the Compatibility Report and note if they are a "square" or "opposition." The orb that you previously calculated applies here as well. If an individual has a Rising Sign that is in aspect by square or opposition, this is an especially heightened indication that the relationship will be disharmonious. Remember, there are fated relationships and those we enter into by choice. If you discover you are in a relationship that is not harmonious, do not panic! If the relationship was fated (mother, father, child) there is a hidden karmic gift. Release your need to control their approach to life, accept that it is appropriate for the development of their spirit in this life. Harmonize on the areas that you can and let everything else go...

* Note: It is worth looking at the location of the Sun and Moon in both charts even if there is a disharmonious relationship between the Ascendants. A good aspect there could help counteract the trouble that would come about if an individual's Ascendant were in one of these three signs.

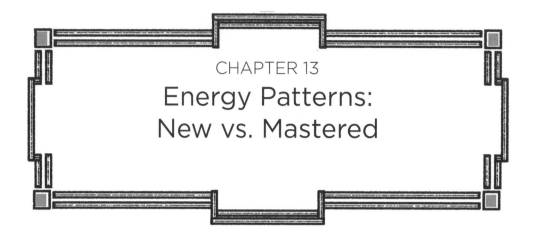

CHAPTER 13
Energy Patterns: New vs. Mastered

POWER PLAN

○ Understand the lesson each planet has to teach us during our earthly incarnation
○ Discover the 4 heightened planetary placements that indicate new versus mastered lessons
○ Learn how to utilize this information to empower yourself

Sometimes it may seem that we are here with the sole experience to be "happy," but the truth is that we are here to experience life—and hopefully with a shift in perception, we learn how to experience life happily, no matter the ups or downs. Through relationships, circumstances, and events we are able to express our unique spirit and continue our internal evolution. We truly are enrolled in a "spiritual school," and as we live our lives, we learn various lessons along the way. Each planet reflects a core lesson that we came here to learn and ultimately master. The planets are our teachers with their own strategy for our spiritual development.

Through the ten core lessons the planets teach, we work our way to higher planes of existence. From how we communicate to our role in relationships, the planets are our coaches, pushing us to achieve all that we can while we are here. As we explore each of these lessons, we will immediately see that these lessons approach our spiritual development in very general terms. This is because one of the most extraordinary aspects of our ability to incarnate on the earth plane is free will. This allows us to learn and express these ten lessons in our own way—none of us are exactly the same. It's as if we all are learning to write, but what we decide to write is ultimately up to us.

Just as one would begin their college education by first working on general education courses, we approach these ten lessons in the exact same manner. After accomplishing the general education portion (practicing the basics of each lesson) we eventually choose a specific "major" or focus in expressing that root lesson through the lives we live. We share the base root of each lesson in common with each other—this is a common theme and exploration for each of us during our earthly experiences. However, once we gain our footing, we channel these lessons in our own beautifully unique way.

The Ten Lessons of the Planets

Sun	Self Expression
Moon	Emotional Intelligence
Mercury	Thinking/Communication
Mars	Right Actions
Venus	Love/Relationships
Jupiter	Spiritual Growth
Saturn	Working for the Good of All
Uranus	Acceptance
Neptune	Empathy
Pluto	Spiritual Ascension

If you are currently incarnated, it goes without saying that you are still working on mastering these lessons—you are, as we all are, a "student" of this world. We spiritually expand by learning and working on these ten core lessons, and this happens through m-u-l-t-i-p-l-e lives. This is something we build on through each incarnation, and it is a continuous process, as we ultimately pick up where we left off in each life. We may excel naturally with certain lessons, but we nevertheless have to express our mastery on the Earth plane before moving upward. Hence, this is why we know that every single person here is working on something. There is no better or worse person—just different stages of spiritual development.

I think it is safe to say that we have all met someone at some point in our life who come across as having it easy. Maybe they were rich, good-looking, smart, charming—whatever trait, it makes no difference. When we witness "success in another," we are experiencing an earthly conundrum. What we cannot fully grasp is that more often than not, these individuals are showing the results of lessons they have practiced through multiple lives. Typically what has happened is that an individual in the current life is simply "remembering" the talents they have developed through m-u-l-t-i-p-l-e lives they have already experienced! For instance, we are all familiar with the musical prodigies that at a young age learned to play the piano in heavenly ways. (Impossible? Yes, in one life it would be, but we don't live just one life.) Those specific skills

were built through multiple lives—they're simply remembering that which they already knew. What appears "easy" is simply a trait "mastered."

With our limited ability to understand the multitude of lives we live, these experiences can be rather confusing, and we can easily go down a dangerous road with how we mentally approach ourselves. Let's face it, we are more likely to beat ourselves up than to actually give ourselves a break—we attack and see ourselves as "less than" when that is not the case. We completely miss out on the truth that the individual was simply "remembering" past talents, skills, and mastered lessons. Whenever this happens and you witness this phenomenon in another, pay honor to the talent or gift that they have. Know deep within yourself that what they are "doing" is something they have practiced through previous incarnations. No one here is better or worse than anyone else—we are all just at varying degrees of our spiritual development. Remind yourself of this often so that you can release yourself from the need to compare yourself to others—there truly is no need.

If you're like me, you will already be asking, "How do I determine which lessons are new to me and which ones are mastered?" We determine this based on where the planets were located in the zodiac at the moment of your birth. There are four heightened positions that each of the planets can take in the zodiac: Rulership, Exaltation, Detriment, and Fall. The moment you were born your spirit was in mathematical harmony with the alignment of the stars. This is why the Natal Chart offers such valuable information on who you are. The physical mirror reflects the physical body, while the Natal Chart reflects the spiritual body. When a planet is in a sign where it is in its Rulership or Exaltation, this is an indication that mastery has been learned on that particular lesson. When a planet is in a sign of its Detriment or Fall, this is an indication that you are approaching a new lesson that requires your attention and patience.

Remember, the ten lessons are general and the expression in the life of the individual is focused. For instance, Johann Sebastian Bach had three planets in Exaltation/Rulership: The Sun in Aries, The Moon in Taurus, and Neptune in Pisces.

The lessons of those planets in which he achieved mastery were: Self Expression, Emotional Intuition, and Empathy. Those lessons lent themselves very well to his ability to create music in a way that stirs the spirit. His ability to compose and bring his vision together at the level in which he did clearly indicates that he was a musician through multiple lives. This isn't to say that when those three planets are in Exaltation/Rulership that it must be expressed through musical mastery—an individual can focus the expression in vastly different ways.

When a planet is in Detriment or Fall, we experience the lower portion of the learning curve—we struggle because it is new, and we are unsure how to actively express that energy on the physical plane. If you have a planet in a heightened location, you most likely won't be surprised by what you discover. These are the gifts and limitations you've come to know all too well. What will happen though, is that you will be provided with an opportunity to strengthen the connection between your spiritual and earthly experiences. You may finally be able to forgive yourself for not being "perfect" because truth be told, none of us are. There is always hidden potential to be unlocked if you have planets in Detriment or Fall because you will be provided with many opportunities to sharpen that skill (more so than if it was in no heightened position at all).

It is vitally important that you have the right frame of mind when exploring this concept. This knowledge can assist you in gaining great clarity, but you must keep an open mind. We must forgive ourselves for not having mastery over every aspect of our lives. Always remind yourself that in our regular daily lives, we understand when we take up a new hobby that we will experience a learning curve. That frustrating time at the beginning is inevitable—it is just part of the learning curve and we accept that as fact. When a planet is in Detriment or Fall, the individual may struggle and experience setbacks because they are still learning. This is okay and all a part of the process. Be patient and empower yourself to do the best you are capable of—nothing more and nothing less.

In this chapter's exercise, you will have an opportunity to determine if any of your planets are in a heightened position. If you have very few

or no planets in heightened positions, that is okay. There are numerous combinations that can occur and none are better or worse than the next. They simply indicate the lessons that are playing an important role in your current incarnation. It is as if you are glancing at your mid-term report card. You have been given the gift of insight and can use the information in a way that allows you to gain a clearer perspective. You are then able to focus in on the areas that require your patience and attention in this life.

Before we jump into the exercise, I would like to illustrate how these lessons can express in an individual's life. If you have ever seen any of Woody Allen's movies, you know that he has one of the most complex and brilliant minds of our time. The raw honesty seen through the neurotic ramblings of his characters illustrates the depths of his own thought processes. Woody Allen has SIX (this is a lot!) planets in heightened positions in his Natal Chart. This is an extraordinary amount of planets and from that information alone we can deduce that there would be a lot of activity and growth going on in his current earthly incarnation.

The three planets that indicated mastery (Rulership and Exaltation) were: Venus, Mars, and Jupiter. These three planets show that he had already laid the groundwork on those lessons of Love/Relationships, Right Actions, and Spiritual Growth. Keep in mind that mastery is not synonymous with perfection. Those with mastery still are capable of channeling the mastery in a direction of their choosing. In this case, he was able to channel his artistic expression in a powerful way through his movies. He had a deep understanding of the complexity of relationships (Venus: Love/Relationship), he knew that he could harness the mental struggles he experienced in the right way (Mars: Right Actions), and he facilitated the opportunity for others to view themselves from a new perspective (Jupiter: Spiritual Growth). Those planets were the key to his ability to produce and create the way that he has. They also allowed him to harness the hidden potential in the other three planets he had located in Detriment/Fall.

For Woody, there was clearly a darker force behind his thinking. It should come as no surprise then that Mercury was located in a heightened position, Detriment. This expressed in the darker exploration of his thought processes and was channeled into his characters. Due to Mars being Exalted, it supported him in choosing the right actions when confronting the darker aspects of the human experience. He was able to tap into that limitation and channel it in a way that allowed him and others to move forward. The other two remaining planets that were in Detriment/Fall: Neptune (Empathy) and Uranus (Acceptance). As you can see, the root of the lesson is what we have in common, but our expression is uniquely "us."

The most important thing to take away from this chapter is rather simple: when we start anything new, we inevitably experience a learning curve. Having the ability to understand that we all must experience the "learning curve," we can release ourselves from being overly self-critical of others and ourselves. If you have struggled with a certain area of your life, try for a moment to release your concept of time. Hold yourself in a space where you can accept that traits are learned over m-u-l-t-i-p-l-e lives, knowing that you are moving forward in perfect timing with your spiritual evolution. Never judge yourself based on another person's set of circumstances, never. If you have been incredibly fortunate and blessed with gifts, do not feel guilty for one minute—you deserve every blessing you have received and even more. If you have struggled with a particular area of your life or personality characteristic, stop beating yourself up! Suspend your concept of living only one life—accept that what you see is not the whole story. Some things are new and some things are mastered and these things take time!

Start Your Exercise!
LIFE LESSONS

Each individual is at a different stage in his or her journey and it's time to figure out what lessons will be capturing your attention in this life.

EXERCISE
Life Lessons

Each of us are students in this "spiritual school." Through the lessons and curriculum of our earthly experience, we will master various lessons until we ascend to a higher plane of existence. The Natal Chart offers valuable information on these lessons and can highlight if any of them are of particular importance in your life.

STEP 1:

Using Table 1 of your Natal Chart Navigator, determine the sign each planet was located in at the moment of your birth. Enter the sign next to the list of planets in the Natal Planet Location to the right.

STEP 2:

Now that you have entered the location of your planets, we need to determine if any of them were located in a heightened position. To the right of the planet list, there are four columns that list the heightened positions for that planet. If the sign you entered matches any of these signs listed, circle the name of the sign in the column.

STEP 3:

Each of the columns (A,B,C & D) represent the four heightened positions a planet can take in the zodiac. If you circled one of these positions, this is a very important lesson for you in this life. The first two columns (A & B) represent Rulership and Exaltation. The last two columns (C & D) represent Detriment and Fall. Looking back to see which planets were in heightened locations, write the name of the planet into the appropriate circles to the right. Remember, Column A & B represent Rulership and Exaltation. Column C & D represent Determine and Fall.

STEP 4:

You have now identified which planets were in heightened locations. Planets that are in Rulership or Exaltation represent lessons you have mastered and indicate areas of your life where you will experience ease. Planets in Detriment or Fall represent lessons you are working on and require your attention. These lessons may be a point of frustration in your life and you must be patient with yourself. The next step is to identify the lessons of each of these planets specifically. In the key below, determine the specific lesson of the planet and enter it below the appropriate circle under "Mastered Lessons" or "New Lessons."

STEP 5:

Take a moment to meditate on what you've discovered. Be thankful for the opportunity to be aware of your past life and progress—know at your core, what is new versus mastered.

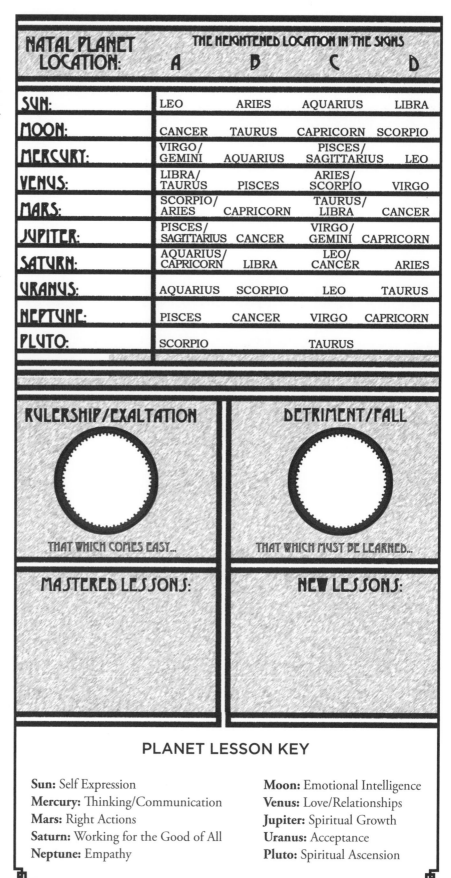

NATAL PLANET LOCATION:	THE HEIGHTENED LOCATION IN THE SIGNS			
	A	B	C	D
SUN:	LEO	ARIES	AQUARIUS	LIBRA
MOON:	CANCER	TAURUS	CAPRICORN	SCORPIO
MERCURY:	VIRGO/ GEMINI	AQUARIUS	PISCES/ SAGITTARIUS	LEO
VENUS:	LIBRA/ TAURUS	PISCES	ARIES/ SCORPIO	VIRGO
MARS:	SCORPIO/ ARIES	CAPRICORN	TAURUS/ LIBRA	CANCER
JUPITER:	PISCES/ SAGITTARIUS	CANCER	VIRGO/ GEMINI	CAPRICORN
SATURN:	AQUARIUS/ CAPRICORN	LIBRA	LEO/ CANCER	ARIES
URANUS:	AQUARIUS	SCORPIO	LEO	TAURUS
NEPTUNE:	PISCES	CANCER	VIRGO	CAPRICORN
PLUTO:	SCORPIO		TAURUS	

RULERSHIP/EXALTATION

THAT WHICH COMES EAST...

DETRIMENT/FALL

THAT WHICH MUST BE LEARNED...

MASTERED LESSONS:

NEW LESSONS:

PLANET LESSON KEY

Sun: Self Expression

Moon: Emotional Intelligence

Mercury: Thinking/Communication

Venus: Love/Relationships

Mars: Right Actions

Jupiter: Spiritual Growth

Saturn: Working for the Good of All

Uranus: Acceptance

Neptune: Empathy

Pluto: Spiritual Ascension

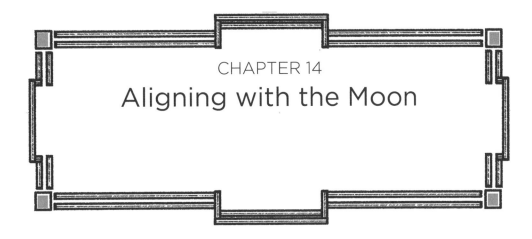

CHAPTER 14
Aligning with the Moon

POWER PLAN

△ Understand why the Moon influences our behaviors and emotions
△ Learn about the waxing and waning phases of the moon
△ Determine how to appropriately time your actions for the best possible outcome

My first understanding of the Moon and its influence was through stories my parents told me as a child. They met while working at a residential treatment facility in Chicago during college and would often reflect back on the experiences they had. One night, they happened to mention something a bit unusual: "We always scheduled extra staff for the night of the Full Moon." I perked up immediately when they said this and, of course, had to ask, "Why? Why would you need more staff on the night of the Full Moon?" And they responded quickly and without hesitation, "Because there was always more action on that day than any other day of the month." And then they would laugh as they continued to share tales of chairs being thrown and outrageous dialogues that took place. I thought it was rather curious that the Moon could have such an effect. I was mesmerized by their stories and that strange fact: that they always scheduled extra staff for the night of the Full Moon.

Later in life, as I began a ten-year stint working in the retail world, I never forgot that bit of information my parents shared with me. Working for a somewhat radical employer, the interaction with customers was pivotal to their understanding of our products. Luckily, many of the individuals I met were eager and happy to share their stories with me and I with them. So any chance I got where I interacted with a doctor, nurse, or counselor, I shared that story from my childhood and waited to hear what they had to say. Each and every time I was affirmed that the Moon did influence the moods and behaviors of people in some way or another. This isn't to say that I think that it is mass hysteria when the Full Moon comes out! I don't believe that at all, but rather I think that some are more susceptible than others to riding its wave. Just as some of us can go on a rocky boat and not be upset by its movement, others will become downright seasick. That is how it goes with the Moon. We will all bend a little bit with its pull and some much more than others.

The Moon has a 28-day cycle and is the fastest of all the cycles you will come to know. It spends roughly 2.5 days in a sign and travels quickly around the entire 12 signs of the zodiac. The phases of the Moon do impact us on a daily basis and this is a great place to start following the energy in your daily life. Many people believe it is the Moon alone that impacts the tides, when in fact that is only half of the equation. It is the magnetic pull between the Sun and Moon that creates the impact we experience on the Earth through the pulling of the tides.

When the Sun and Moon are directly across from each other in the zodiac, we experience a Full Moon in the night sky. The light from the Sun is completely absorbed and reflected back to us from the Moon. This is when the magnetic pull is at its strongest because they are directly across from each other. Think about this for just a minute. If this magnetic pull can influence the movement of the tides, isn't it worth entertaining the notion that it might have an effect on us? The Full Moon is known for its social nature and for providing a great time for gatherings and social events of all kinds. It is a time where people shut down their inner filters and "live and let live." Sometimes this means that some will act a little bizarre or start saying things without thinking.

The Moon in astrology represents the feminine energy that is deeply nurturing and caring. It is an intuitive and instinctual part of who we are and the "us" that has no filter. The Sun represents the masculine energy with its drive to do and achieve (the ego). You can imagine then how this interaction between the masculine and feminine energies within us is so affected by this Moon cycle. The two weeks leading up to the Full Moon (waxing phases) is the extroverted and outward portion of this energy cycle. The two weeks where it returns to the New Moon (waning phases) is the restorative and internal energy portion. The internal pull is always at its strongest the week before the

New Moon. And this is how the cycle continues on—inward and outward, over and over again.

When the Moon passes in front of the Sun (same sign and degree in the zodiac), we experience a New Moon. The energy leading up to the New Moon is very different than that of a Full Moon. This is a time where you are most likely not feeling an urge to interact with the world. There is a definite inward pull during this period to spend time alone or to surround yourself by those closest to you. The energy of the New Moon is one that is often harder for people to embrace because we live in a world that doesn't want to slow down on any level. Back when there were no bright city lights keeping the world awake for hours after sunset, without the Moon's glow, people would naturally hole up and spend time at home.

During the waning phases, if you are unable to provide this resting time for yourself, you will most likely find yourself agitated and short tempered as the New Moon approaches each month. This is never the ideal time to be starting new projects, sending out job resumes, or going on a first date. Think of the waning phases of the moon as the "inhale" of the breath and the waxing phases of the moon as the "exhale." It is not possible to blow up the balloon on the "inhale" (waning phases), you can only do that on the "exhale" (waxing phases).

When I first began exploring, I wanted to put this "Moon magic" to work in my life. With Capricorn Rising, I am always seeking "to utilize" the information that is given to me (personal power phrase of Capricorn). I happened to be a retail manager at a very busy shop when I discovered how I could align myself with the Moon. One day I eagerly decided that I would schedule my shop's activities to the phases of the Moon for a little experiment. There were many things I was responsible for through managing my shop, and I was excited to have such a platform to put these theories to work in. From staff meetings to job fairs, I decided to see if the Moon could help. I knew from my studies that the Full Moon was a time for socializing and trying something new, and that sounded like the perfect energy for a successful job fair when it came to my line of work.

Envision the Full Moon and New Moon as mere turning points in an energetic flow that is very much like the breath. When I required the strongest energy that each of these cycles supported, I would focus on being within three days of these turning points in the relevant phase (waxing or waning) that could support my goal. I decided to give myself a buffer when working with the Moon and decided it was okay to provide a bit of space around the actual Full or New Moon for scheduling my activities. In the case of my job fairs, I planned them any time of the week leading up to the Full Moon to catch the energy that would be pulsating at those times. I was blown away by the results. I went from job fairs that on a good day would have eight to ten people, to job fairs where over twenty-plus individuals showed up. I didn't have enough chairs! It was like magic. All I had to do was honor the energy and divine flow that lives in us all and my results were changing.

Because of these Moon experiments, I kept to watching the phases and timing my actions as best as I could. The Moon not only taught me when to do things, but it also taught me when not to do things. I avoided many things the week before a New Moon: staff meetings, job fairs, parties, events, etc. My take was: Why should I schedule something at a possibly inopportune time? It took very little effort to pull up a Moon phase calendar and make sure I avoided those dates. I figured if I could get the cosmos on my side it was worth a shot! Whether you are skeptical or not, it certainly will not hurt you to conduct a little bit of an experiment when it comes to this "Moon magic." Whether that means you begin to consciously choose when to submit a resume or when you choose to start a new project, the Moon can always help you get your best results. Follow the phases of the Moon by accessing the Moon Phase Calendar at www.absolutelyastrology.com.

I did make a few pivotal mistakes when I conducted my Moon experiments. My first mistake was that I felt everything I was trying to accomplish would be assisted best during the waxing phases of the Moon. Initially, I believed that nearly any endeavor would prosper best under the waxing phases, but I soon discovered this was inaccurate! The waxing phases are about adding to our lives and the waning phases are for release and letting go. I had started a fruit cleanse at the beginning of a New Moon and was rewarded by gaining 5 pounds. I literally could not believe it because I had made significantly positive changes to what I was eating! The thing of it is, the waxing phases help us add things into our lives and the waning phases help us release unwanted things back into the universal pool. A diet or cleanse started during the waxing phases will have a different effect than one started during the waning phases. The best time to break a habit or release things unwanted is always better supported during the waning phases of the Moon.

The exercise for this chapter is truly an opportunity to align your goals with the cyclical nature of the Moon. Start very simple and see if it makes a difference in your life. All you need to do is remember that the extroverted time of this cycle is when the Moon is waxing (moving from the New Moon to the Full Moon). Conversely, the inward time starts during the waning phases (Full Moon back to New Moon) and is at its peak that week just before the New Moon. During the waxing phases, it is about adding more to your life and moving forward. The waning phases support letting go of what no longer serves to lighten your load energetically and to clear space. There are so many unseen forces at play in our environment. What a gift it is that astrology can help us decipher how to work with them.

There are many who follow the Moon in great detail, but I prefer to loosely align with its pull through the basic two phases: waning and waxing. It is my personal opinion that the more we gravitate towards micro-managing and rigidness in our application of astrology, the more we actually begin to lose sight of the bigger goal. Often in these cases, we are energetically trying to force things and that almost always works against our true intentions.

My advice is to view this as a greater pattern and essentially the "spiritual breath" of our Oneness, The Universe or God. When we approach the moon in this manner, it is just like we are hitching a ride with the great cosmic forces. When we are in the "exhale" (the waxing phases), we are in manifestation and creation mode. When we are in the "inhale" (the waning phases), we are in release and reflection mode. My philosophy on the application of astrology is to use it as a tool in conjunction with your natural intuition. Don't over-think it; just align with the general pull and let the cosmos do the rest.

Waning = Inhale = Internal
Waxing = Exhale = Extrovert

Start Your Exercise!
MOON PLANNER

We begin now to find practical ways to embrace the influence and rhythm of the cosmos through aligning with the Moon.

EXERCISE
Moon Planner

In this exercise we will begin to explore the dynamic power the Moon holds over the success you have in accomplishing your goals. Before completing this exercise, you will need to gain access to a Moon Phase calendar. Please visit www.absolutelyastrology.com to view the current and upcoming phases of the Moon. This exercise can be repeated as many times as you would like, so if you're anticipating using it multiple times, please photocopy prior to completing.

STEP 1:

Regardless of what phase the Moon is in at the time you are completing this exercise, you are absolutely capable of immediately aligning with its energetic pull.

In the circles labeled Goal 1, 2 & 3 on the left bottom of the Moon Planner worksheet, fill in 3 goals or activities that you would like to accomplish in the next 30 days. Choose anything that is relevant in your life currently. There is no action too small or too big for aligning with the power of the Moon.

STEP 2:

There are two specific energetic patterns present through the cyclical nature of the Moon: the waning phases (Full Moon to New Moon) and the waxing phases (New Moon to Full Moon). The charts on the right of the worksheet will explain the dynamics present and the possible activities that will likely have a beneficial outcome when performed during those specific phases. The success you have in achieving the goals you created depends on numerous factors, but the energy of the Moon can either support or hinder the success of these goals.

1. Based on the table and examples to the right, determine whether the goal you are trying to achieve is best suited for either the waxing or waning phases of the Moon.

2. Enter either waning or waxing in the box connected to the specific goal you are analyzing.

STEP 3:

Once you determine the Moon Phase that is most appropriate for your goal/activity, look to the Moon Phase calendar to pick the date that you will either begin or complete the activity listed.

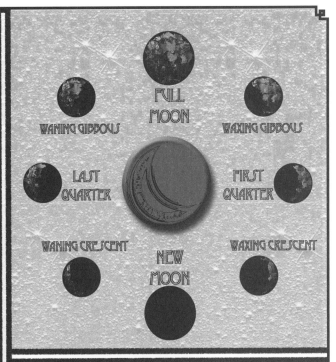

WANING GIBBOUS — FULL MOON — WAXING GIBBOUS

LAST QUARTER — FIRST QUARTER

WANING CRESCENT — NEW MOON — WAXING CRESCENT

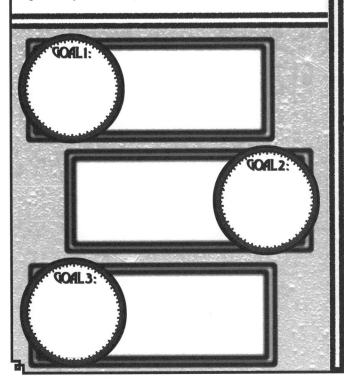

GOAL 1:

GOAL 2:

GOAL 3:

NEW MOON - FULL MOON (WAXING PHASES)

THE WAXING PHASES OF THE MOON ARE AN EXTERNAL AND EXTROVERTED TIME. THIS IS WHEN YOU WILL BE REWARDED FOR SOCIAL ENDEAVORS AND STARTING NEW PROJECTS THAT CAN PROPEL YOUR LIFE FORWARD. THIS IS A TIME PERIOD WHERE IT IS EASIEST TO ADD ON NEW AND FUN ENERGY TO YOUR LIFE.

START A NEW PROJECT
BEGIN A NEW STUDY
GO SHOPPING
TRAVEL FOR PLEASURE
START A NEW JOB
BUY SOMETHING NEW
TRAIN SOMEONE
BEGIN A SAVINGS ACCT
THROW A PARTY
FIX SOMETHING
DIET - TO GAIN WEIGHT
COLLECT A DEBT
BEAUTY TREATMENT

BREAK A BAD HABIT
TRAVEL FOR REFLECTION
DIET - TO LOSE WEIGHT
CANNING OF FOOD
PLANT SEEDS
READ A BOOK
MEDITATION
BORROW MONEY
START THERAPY
GET A MASSAGE
START A CLEANSE
CLEAN YOUR HOUSE

FULL MOON - NEW MOON (WANING PHASES)

THE WANING PHASES OF THE MOON ARE A TIME FOR REFLECTION AND ARE HIGHLY INTROVERTED. THIS IS A TIME TO RELEASE AND LET GO OF THAT WHICH NO LONGER SERVES YOU. ANYTHING THAT YOU WOULD LIKE TO SAY GOODBYE TO OR RELEASE BACK TO THE WORLD CAN BEST BE DONE NOW.

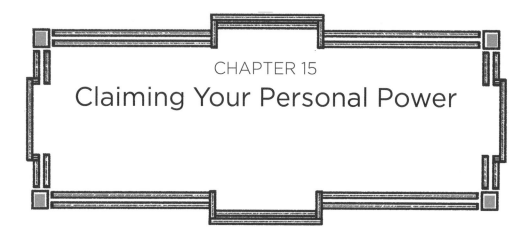

CHAPTER 15

Claiming Your Personal Power

POWER PLAN

△ Determine the three major tipping-point years of your life
△ Discover how to claim your power
△ Construct your official Natal Chart

It may seem backwards to share my story with you now as you come to the final chapter of this book. As I mentioned in the first chapter, I was always a very different child, unique and intense. My story of spiritual awakening is interlaced with the events and circumstance of my life, but if you were to sift out the most powerful moments—from the night I saw a ghost at the foot of my bed to the moment I arrived in a state of absolute acceptance of the unseen—there were tipping-point-moments. Times where the stars aligned and set me on my right path. I believe we all have these moments in our lives, where we are presented with uncommon circumstances, events or insights, but it is up to us—we have to choose to lead with our heart, to ultimately claim our power.

One of those tipping-point-moments came when I was in college. One day I awoke to the feeling of energy running through my back, a sensation so powerful that the warm tingling followed me wherever I went. A few weeks later, I began to see auras. I knew that my life perception was being called to a higher level and I was scared.

I frantically searched the web to figure out my symptoms. I came quickly to the realization that I was experiencing a Kundalini Awakening, and although I should have been validated, all I felt was an even deeper confusion. According to my research, my "subtle body" had become awakened and what I felt in my back was the energy that moves through us all.

The experience of feeling energy is vastly different for each individual—it is as unique to the individual as the individual is unique. For me, the awakening of the Kundalini felt much like my feet feel when they have fallen asleep. It is a distinct sensation of energy in the physical body; it was confusing, different, and it grabbed my attention. At least, that was how it all started during my initial phase of awakening. Once I had finally reached a place of deciphering what was happening, I began to see auras (or my version of auras). For me, seeing auras was extremely simplified comparative to what others have described. I began to see two different obvious hues and those with the undeniable golden/amber hue radiating from them always became of great importance in my life. But I'm getting ahead of myself, because I must stress, as this all began to unfold, I was filled with anxiety, fear, and at some points even denial.

These awakenings can happen for many reasons: emotional trauma, major life events, deep meditation and practice, and seemingly from out of nowhere. Mine was from an emotional trauma that shattered me. But as I look back now—the path makes sense; it didn't then…

It's interesting because on the one hand, I was so entranced by everything happening—the feeling of energy circulating through me, seeing people's auras, and knowing so much intuitively about who they were. On the other hand, I was terrified that I might be losing my mind. I could see people and focus in on who they really were, the "unseen them." It was a latent gift waiting to evolve and if I had been more present, I would have seen that it was evident from a young age. I had been told so many times that I had that effect that when I looked at someone, they could feel me staring into their soul.

When I was in grade school, kids ran away from me on the playground because of my "piercing" eyes. Once, when I was a retail manager, I even had someone drop off a resume to me with their hand covering their face, telling me they couldn't "look into my eyes." My latent gift had been awakened, and I was experiencing a physical spiritual awakening, a tipping-point-moment I had craved my whole life, but I was too afraid to let go of the "truths" my mind had accepted as fact.

My heart had always embraced taking on this spiritual journey, but my mind fought viciously to keep me from moving out of "its" reality. When I experienced the intense physical part of my awakening in college, I felt like I had a secret and I became anxious all the time. I was only twenty-one years old, and in so many ways, I didn't know who I was yet. I tried channeling that energy into a new desire by leaving town, and I abruptly moved abroad to England for my final semester. When I arrived in London, my mind coped by producing an excessive amount of thought and bounced back and forth between acceptance and complete denial. I had what I always wanted—a spiritual awakening on the physical plane (feeling energy and seeing auras)—but I was still so fearful of losing my sanity that I could hardly enjoy the process that had begun. It was as if I couldn't let go of the reality I had been programmed to accept, no matter how much I wanted to fully believe and live my life from the vantage point of spirit.

It wasn't until one fateful day when my sister gifted me my first Natal Chart reading that my heart began to steer my life and my mind finally believed. Nancy Murdock-Gulliksen, who provided me with my first astrological reading and who later became my mentor, opened the session with, "Are you a published author?" I was blown away. That was my dream of all dreams that I had tucked away and silently wished for since I was in fourth grade. At that moment, I wasn't a published author. It was simply one of my foolish dreams. How could she have known that or seen that as an option for me? She continued to provide me with profound knowledge that could only have come from a deeper source. Another tipping-point-moment had shown up in my life, but this time I claimed it. She spoke to the unseen me with complete accuracy and all I needed to do was to lean ever so slightly into that knowing. I believed with my mind and my heart—I began to follow the path I had always wanted for myself in this life.

If you were to ask me when this spiritual journey clicked and came together for me, I would say, "It was absolutely astrology." From that moment when I was truly seen, all doubt was washed away from my mind. The universal intelligence that is in all things, spoke to me that day through its native tongue: astrology. I was able to claim my power and live authentically from the vantage point of spirit—no longer frightened of becoming more. There was no epic battle between my heart and mind to distract me. They had finally formed the kindred friendship that I had yearned for all along.

We are just as the seed. We must find our light, and no one else can do this for us. (As much as I had wished some wise elder would have shown up at my doorstep, that isn't how these things work.) We have to claim our power and actively move ourselves forward—bridging the gaps, tightening the bond between mind, body, and spirit. Through the moments you have experienced you have moved closer and closer to this deeper understanding. You have been presented with your own tipping-point-moments and perhaps this is one for you right now.

For me, I found and fell in love with astrology. I didn't have much money at the time, and I walked to the library every week and read every book they had available. In fact, I ordered books from all the branches of the local libraries until I was repeating myself. I eventually reached a point where there was no more I could learn from a book—and as fate would have it, money was finding its way back to me. At that time I decided to reach out and find a mentor because I was ready to learn. I knew I had reached a point where I had done all the work I was capable of on my own.

That was when I reached out to Nancy (who gave me my first reading at the age of thirty) and asked if she would take me on as a student. She, in her habit of watching the astrological cycles, received her own validation—a Jupiter transit return and an unfolding she had witnessed 12 years before that was happening to her yet again. I had essentially shown up at her doorstep asking to be taught at the exact right time. She accepted me as a student (of course after looking back at my chart to make sure we were a good match—a true astrologer).

I was blessed, I was fortunate, and she took me on as a student. I know now that this is not the first time Nancy has been my mentor, teacher, and friend. I'm not sure through how many lifetimes this wonderful spirit and soul has assisted me, but I'm forever grateful and she undoubtedly changed my life this time around and perhaps all the rest. I realized something very powerful as this all unfolded: we are all student and teacher simultaneously—what I've learned I can teach, but I will never be done learning. You as well are both a student and a teacher. Claim your power by being both. You deserve a mentor, teacher, and friend who will assist you as you walk down your path. (We all do, and I wish I would have believed that I was worthy much sooner.) When we learn to share our gifts freely and we equally learn to eagerly receive from a place of appreciation, we will support each other towards our common goal—living in light and love.

I think back to that scared little girl in college who was so confused and afraid of letting go and believing. I wish I could declare to her that everything she was experiencing was real. That she was experiencing a beautiful unfolding of spirit, fully waking up in the physical body. I want to tell her that this happens quickly and yet so slowly, but that it is worth the struggle to push through. I would say, do not give up. Keep going. Keep looking forward and choosing your heart over your mind—I would say that the unseen is more real than she could ever imagine and that she should not be afraid of her light. I would say that she is special, that we all are. That each person has greatness to contribute to the world and the biggest enemy is overcoming the self-doubt we inevitably face.

My hope is that many of you are simply blown away by the insight and direction available to you through astrology. I hope that you had moments where your jaw dropped and you couldn't believe how this book was able to see you, the real you. And to the few who perhaps didn't experience that—all I can say is, check your birth time. Please, check your birth time. Astrology is never wrong.

Your Natal Chart has the ability to validate all that you have always known about yourself and it can remind you of who you really are. In this final exercise, we will create your official Natal Chart—drawing all the concepts together. We will also introduce one final concept that can allow you to pinpoint when you will receive the most powerful tipping-point-moments of your life. There is a technique that astrologers use to predict how each year of your life will develop and this is called the Progressed Chart. When you were born, the Sun was in a specific location within the zodiac at a specific degree. For every degree the Sun moved after the day of your birth, it depicts the development of your consciousness, year-by-year, one degree for one year.

You will experience many tipping-point-moments in your life, but none will surpass the energy that surrounds you on the years that your progressed Sun changes zodiac signs. As I stated previously, for every degree the Sun moves forward after the moment of your birth, it holds influence over your life and development of self. If you were born with your Sun at 10°Pisces, at the age of 20 you would experience your first tipping-point year. This is because each sign has 30 degrees and each degree counts as one year of your life. If your Sun was at 10°Pisces, and every sign has 30 degrees, it would take 20 degrees (20 years) before you entered the next sign. In that case, the progressed Sun would be moving from Pisces into Aries when the individual was 20 years old.

These years are powerful and can propel you forward into a new state of consciousness previously unavailable to you. In the case of the Sun, which was at 10°Pisces, that first tipping-point year happened at 20 years of age. The second tipping-point year would happen at 50 years of age, when the progressed Sun entered the sign of Taurus (30 years added to the first tipping-point year). We can continue to add 30 years (essentially 30 degrees/one sign) to discover all of the tipping-point years of a life, but the first three are the most pivotal. In this case, the three tipping points ages are 20/50/80.

In the exercise, you will discover the three most powerful tipping-point years of your life. My first tipping-point-year was when I was 27, and this age perfectly correlates with my engagement and marriage to my husband, Adam. That year marked the beginning of a brand-new stage for me. It was the first time I was actually willing to truly lay down roots, and it was that very act that finally allowed me to grow.

Remember, there will always be other tipping-point-moments, but that these three years of age will stand above the rest. They will mark the three most transformative years of your life, where you can pick up speed and rise into new levels of consciousness. All you have to do is choose to actively arrive; show up and claim your power. Astrology is a profound tool that is always ready to help you succeed, gain insight, and grow you to your full potential. You simply need to embrace the knowledge and use it wisely with love.

Through this spiritual journey, you have discovered many things you already knew and perhaps some things you had forgotten. You know now what your spiritual direction is for this life and what you came here to learn. You know the specific goal you set for yourself and what you are trying to achieve. You've witnessed the unseen forces and have been invited to now consciously align yourself with their influence. You know that you are not your physical body, but the essence within. You are complex, beautiful, and in a constant state of becoming. You've received the gift of your very own tipping-point-moment.

Remember, there is no circumstance from which you cannot recover. There is no life so broken that it cannot be fixed and put to its right path. There is no depression so deep that you cannot find one glimmer of light to lead you back. You have more support pulling you forward than you could ever know, but you have to claim your power. You must act in ways that allow for this to unfold—you must follow your inspiration, destiny, and purpose. No other person in this world is like you; no one else has the life circumstance to realize the intention you set forth for your life.

There should never be a divide from the person you dream about being and the person that you truly are. Each of us incarnated for a specific reason and each of us has something beautiful to add to this world. Live the life you were meant to live. Claim your power. Decide today—right in this very moment—you are worth believing in. We all are.

Start Your Exercise!
COMPLETING YOUR NATAL CHART

We have now reached the culminating moment of this spiritual journey. Discover the most powerful tipping-point-years of your life—and take the steps necessary to claim your power.

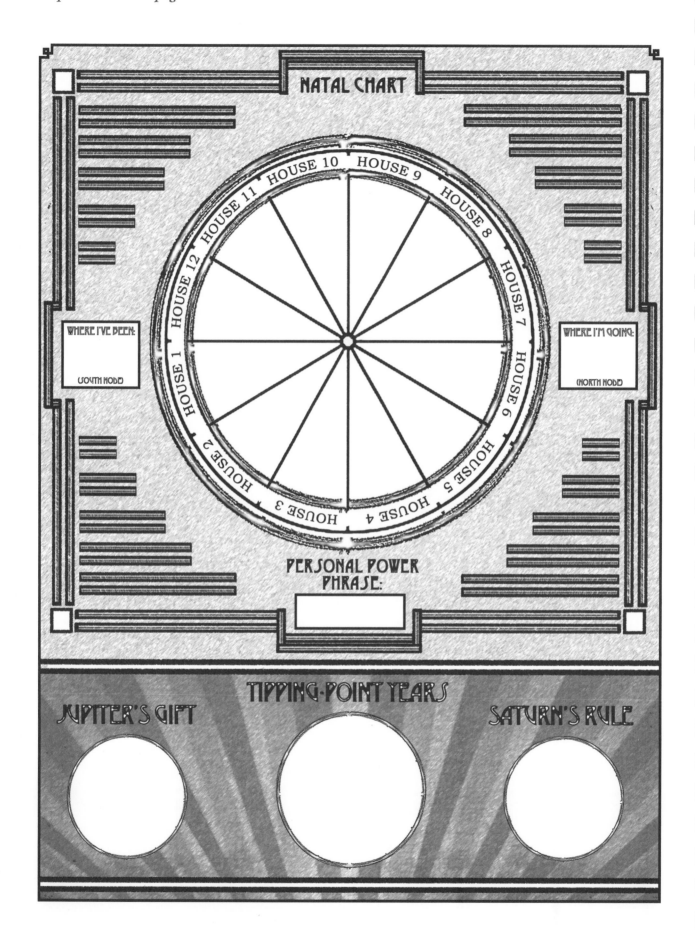

NATAL CHART

WHERE I'VE BEEN:

(SOUTH NODE)

WHERE I'M GOING:

(NORTH NODE)

HOUSE 10 · HOUSE 9 · HOUSE 11 · HOUSE 8 · HOUSE 12 · HOUSE 7 · HOUSE 1 · HOUSE 6 · HOUSE 2 · HOUSE 5 · HOUSE 3 · HOUSE 4

PERSONAL POWER PHRASE:

TIPPING-POINT YEARS

JUPITER'S GIFT

SATURN'S RULE

EXERCISE
Completing Your Natal Chart

It's now time to put together all of the insights you have discovered through this spiritual journey in your official Natal Chart. May it serve as deep validation and inspiration to your spirit.

Start by writing your name just below the words "Natal Chart" on the worksheet.

STEP 1:

1. The most important thing to remember as you move forward is the spiritual direction of your life. For that information, we look to the Moon Nodes and the insights we discovered in chapter 3. Looking back to that exercise, determine the quadrants where your South and North Node are located. In the Moon Node key at the bottom boxes of the worksheet, a key word has been selected for each quadrant. In the box on the left side of your Natal Chart; enter the key word for the quadrant for where you've been (South Node).

2. In the box on the right side of your Natal Chart, enter the key word for where you're going (North Node).

STEP 2:

Every person has a personal power phrase that ignites the flame of their soul's purpose. In chapter 5, you discovered your personal power phrase based on your Rising Sign. There is a key of these personal power phrases in the bottom left box of the worksheet. Enter your personal power phrase into the box below your Natal Chart.

STEP 3:

It's now time to enter the location of each planet at the moment of your birth. This part of the exercise can be done in any way that specifically inspires YOU. The symbols for the signs and planets are located in the keys in the bottom right boxes of the worksheet. You can choose to use some of the symbols or none of the symbols, this is completely up to you. Using Table 1 of your Natal Chart Navigator, enter the location of each planet, degree, and sign into the appropriate house.

STEP 4:

There is something that your soul craves, a deeper want that drives your life forward—the Part of Fortune. Enter the location of your Part of Fortune from The Fortunes worksheet into the appropriate house of your Natal Chart.

STEP 5:

Right now at this very moment, Jupiter is supporting your spiritual expansion and abundance. In chapter 11 you discovered which house Jupiter is currently transiting in your chart. Remember, it takes 12 years for Jupiter to transit around your chart and it is a very powerful force to align yourself with—pay attention to its journey. Looking back to the exercise from chapter 11, enter the current house and life experience Jupiter is supporting into the blank circle below your Natal Chart called Jupiter's Gift.

STEP 6:

Saturn is providing structure to the development of your life. Through the four phases of its cycle, you are able to gain valuable information into how your life will unfold. Beneath the Natal Chart, there is a circle for Saturn's Rule. Look back to chapter 10 to determine the current phase Saturn is in for your life. Enter the phase and description into this circle. For example: Phase 1: Take Off and Climb, Phase 2: Cruising Altitude, Phase 3: Final Descent, Phase 4: Landing.

STEP 7:

It is now time to determine the three most powerful tipping point years of your life. To calculate these years, we will do the math by hand below.

In Table 1 of your Natal Chart Navigator, determine the degree of your Natal Sun. You can enter this number into the circle just below X=degree of Natal Sun. This will be used as the "X" in the first equation (complete all equations now). Please note, each number you calculate gets used in the following equation. Once you complete the math, the three numbers you entered represent three different years of age—these three specific ages mark the most powerful tipping point years of your life. Enter them into the blank middle circle beneath your Natal Chart.

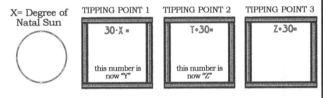

X= Degree of Natal Sun

TIPPING POINT 1
$$30 - X =$$
this number is now "Y"

TIPPING POINT 2
$$Y + 30 =$$
this number is now "Z"

TIPPING POINT 3
$$Z + 30 =$$

STEP 8:

It's time to claim your power and to trust your instincts. Move forward confidently and in alignment with your true spiritual purpose. IF this book moved you, please pay it forward so that more people may claim their power. Thank you from my heart for allowing me to be your guide on this spiritual journey. *In light and love, Emily*

MOON NODE

Quadrant 1:
Self/Independence

Quadrant 2:
Private/Family

Quadrant 3:
Relationships

Quadrant 4:
Public/Leader

POWER PHRASE

Aries: I Am
Taurus: I Have
Gemini: I Think
Cancer: I Feel
Leo: I Will
Virgo: I Know
Libra: I Balance
Scorpio: I Desire
Sagittarius: I Aim
Capricorn: I Utilize
Aquarius: I Know
Pisces: I Believe

GLYPH FOR SIGN

♈ Aries
♉ Taurus
♊ Gemini
♋ Cancer
♌ Leo
♍ Virgo
♎ Libra
♏ Scorpio
♐ Sagittarius
♑ Capricorn
♒ Aquarius
♓ Pisces

GLYPH FOR PLANET

☉ Sun
☽ Moon
☿ Mercury
♀ Venus
♂ Mars
♃ Jupiter
♄ Saturn
♅ Uranus
♆ Neptune
♇ Pluto
⊗ Part of Fortune

Bibliography

Hand, Robert. *Planets in Transit, Life Cycles for Living.* Pennsylvania, 1976.

Holt, Rinehart, and Winstin. *Astrology for Adults.* Canada: Holt, 1969.

Lewi, Grant. *Astrology for the Millions.* Garden City Publishing, 1942.

March, Marion D., and Joan McEvers. *The Only Way to Learn Astrology, Volume 1: Basic Principles.* Canada: Astro-Analytic Publications, 1976.

— *The Only Way to Learn Astrology, Volume 2: Math and Interpretation Technique.* Canada: Astro-Analytic Publications, 1977.

— *The Only Way to Learn Astrology, Volume 3: Horoscope Analysis.* San Diego: ACS Publications, 1988.

Schulman, Martin. *Karmic Astrology, Volume 1.* Maine: Samuel Weiser, 1975.

Spiller, Jan. *New Moon Astrology.* New York: Bantam Books, 2001

Stearn, Jess. *A Time for Astrology.* New York: Longmans Canada Limited, 1971.

Tierney, Bill. *All Around the Zodiac, Exploring Astrology's 12 Signs.* Minnesota: Llewellyn Publications, 2004.

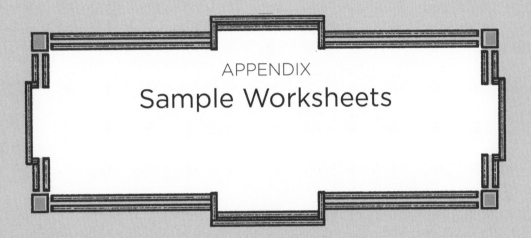

APPENDIX

Sample Worksheets

EXERCISE
Element & Mode Exploration

Each sign in the zodiac is the combination of an element and mode. In the four rectangles below the circle, the signs have been sorted by element: Fire, Earth, Air, and Water. Each mode for the specific sign is also listed just below its name: Cardinal, Fixed, and Mutable. Follow the steps to complete this first exercise. There is a sample worksheet for you to reference as you complete each exercise located in the Appendix (the page number is referenced at the top of each worksheet).

STEP 1:
The circle on the worksheet is divided into quadrants. Each quadrant represents an element: Fire, Earth, Air, and Water.
The 4 blocks below the element and mode circle show the elements with their appropriate signs.

1. Using Table 1 in your Natal Chart Navigator, look at each planet in column 1 and its matching sign in column 2.

2. Using the table, look at the 4 element boxes on the worksheet to see which planet should be written in each quadrant of the circle. (For example: if your Sun is in Pisces, the boxes below the circle show Pisces in the Water element box. Write Sun in the Water quadrant of the large circle.) This shows where each sign was when you were born.

3. Once you look up each sign to discover the element and mode activated and have written the planet into the element circle at the top, tally the mode in the bottom boxes. (The modes are shown in the element boxes below each sign. Use the key box below to check off each planet as you go.

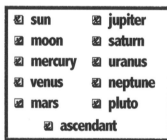

STEP 2:
1. Look to see which element and mode is strongest in your chart by adding up the totals.

2. Once they have been discovered, write them into the circles below entitled Strongest Element and Strongest Mode. You can read more about the elements/modes in this chapter for further insight.

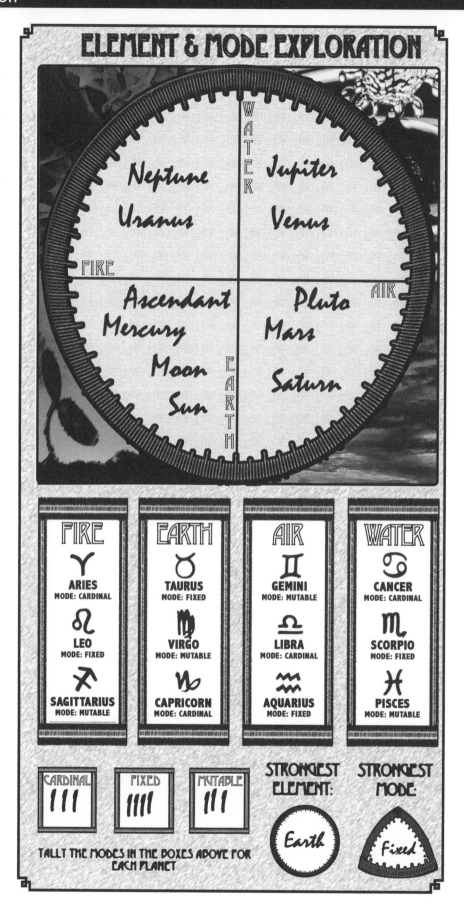

POWER CLUSTERS & HOUSE EXPLORATION

IN THIS EXERCISE WE WILL BEGIN TO EXPLORE THE ARCHETYPES RULING EACH OF YOUR HOUSES AND WE WILL DISCOVER IF THERE ARE ANY POWER CLUSTERS PRESENT.

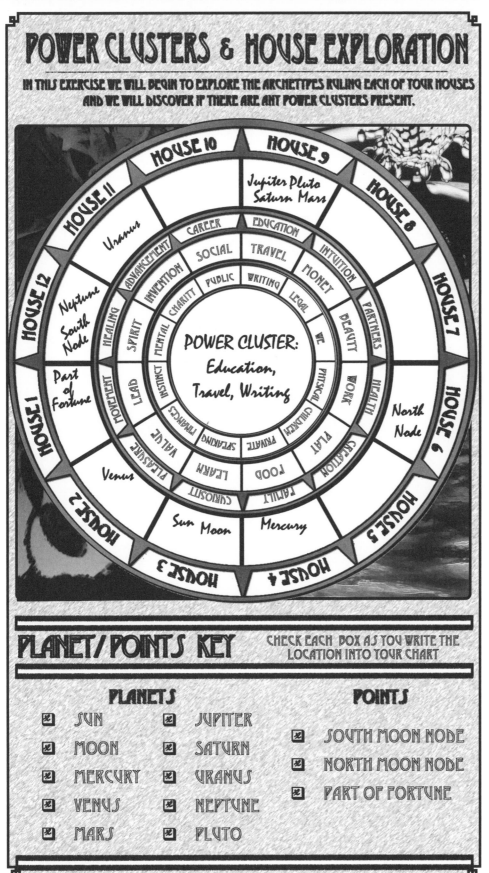

PLANET/POINTS KEY

CHECK EACH BOX AS YOU WRITE THE LOCATION INTO YOUR CHART

PLANETS

- ☒ SUN
- ☒ MOON
- ☒ MERCURY
- ☒ VENUS
- ☒ MARS
- ☒ JUPITER
- ☒ SATURN
- ☒ URANUS
- ☒ NEPTUNE
- ☒ PLUTO

POINTS

- ☒ SOUTH MOON NODE
- ☒ NORTH MOON NODE
- ☒ PART OF FORTUNE

The circle to the right shows each of the 12 Astrological Houses in Astrology. Within the circle are three words that describe the dynamics at play in each house. Please ensure you have your Natal Chart Navigator ready to complete the following steps.

STEP 1:

Now it's time to write the planet/points of your Natal Chart into the Astrological Houses.

Look to Table 1 in your Natal Chart Navigator to determine the house location for each planet in column 4. Utilize the Planet/Points Key to keep track as you enter each Planet/Point into the chart.

* Please note that you will not enter the Ascendant

STEP 2:

If you have three or more planets in a house, you have a "Power Cluster." This is an indication of a strong focused energy in that area of your life. The words on the innermost portion of the circle reflect what areas of your life this focused energy will be affecting.

If you identified a power cluster in your chart, write "Power Cluster" in the blank innermost circle along with the three words listed for that house. If you did not discover a power cluster in your chart, write "jack of all trades" into the middle circle.

Discover your approach to life through the distribution of the planets in the Astrological Houses. Do you have a Power Cluster? Or have you chosen a jack-of-all-trades approach?

EXERCISE
Fate vs. Free Will

NOW IT IS TIME TO DISCOVER THE INFLUENCES OF FATE AND FREE WILL IN YOUR LIFE. REMEMBER, THERE
WILL BE FATED MOMENTS THROUGHOUT YOUR ENTIRE LIFE. HOW YOU REACT AND THE
ROAD YOU CHOOSE EACH TIME IS ULTIMATELY UP TO YOU.
CHOOSE WISELY

STEP 1:
Looking back to the last exercise, determine the number of planets and sensitive points in each house.

STEP 2:
Write each number into the inner circle and the correct house on the worksheet detailing the discovery of the influences of fate and free will in your life.

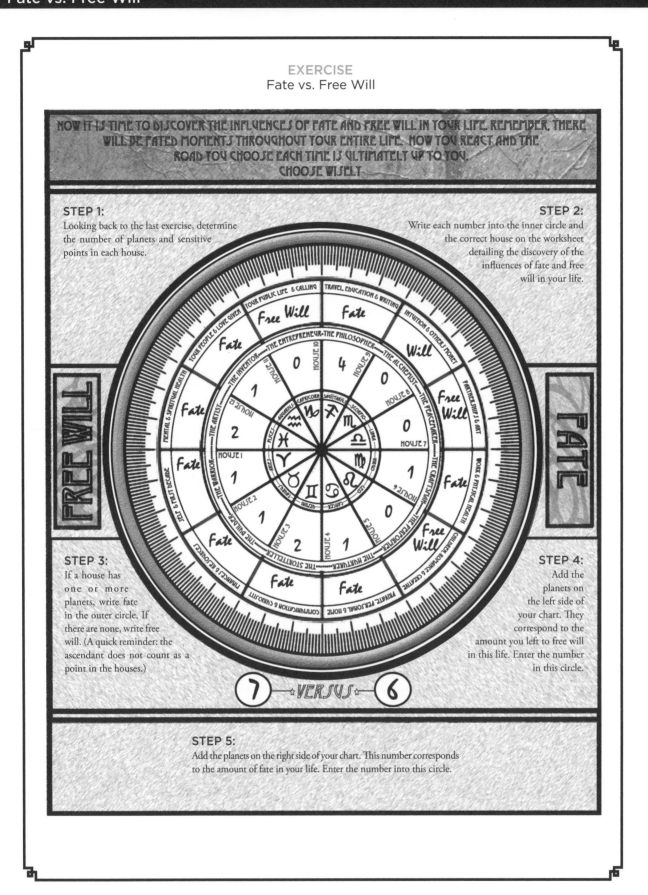

STEP 3:
If a house has one or more planets, write fate in the outer circle. If there are none, write free will. (A quick reminder: the ascendant does not count as a point in the houses.)

STEP 4:
Add the planets on the left side of your chart. They correspond to the amount you left to free will in this life. Enter the number in this circle.

STEP 5:
Add the planets on the right side of your chart. This number corresponds to the amount of fate in your life. Enter the number into this circle.

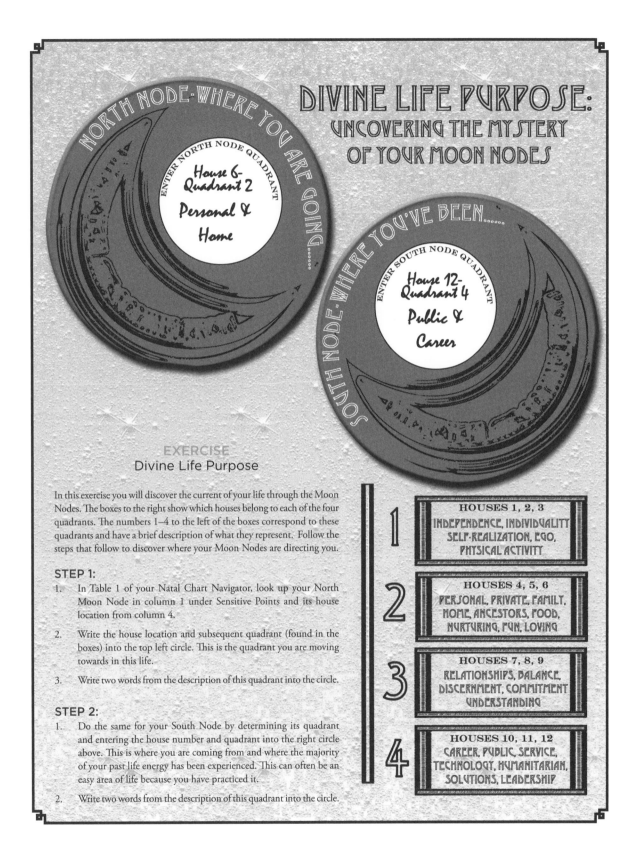

NORTH NODE-WHERE YOU ARE GOING

DIVINE LIFE PURPOSE:
UNCOVERING THE MYSTERY OF YOUR MOON NODES

ENTER NORTH NODE QUADRANT

House 6-
Quadrant 2
Personal &
Home

SOUTH NODE-WHERE YOU'VE BEEN...

ENTER SOUTH NODE QUADRANT

House 12-
Quadrant 4
Public &
Career

EXERCISE
Divine Life Purpose

In this exercise you will discover the current of your life through the Moon Nodes. The boxes to the right show which houses belong to each of the four quadrants. The numbers 1–4 to the left of the boxes correspond to these quadrants and have a brief description of what they represent. Follow the steps that follow to discover where your Moon Nodes are directing you.

STEP 1:

1. In Table 1 of your Natal Chart Navigator, look up your North Moon Node in column 1 under Sensitive Points and its house location from column 4.

2. Write the house location and subsequent quadrant (found in the boxes) into the top left circle. This is the quadrant you are moving towards in this life.

3. Write two words from the description of this quadrant into the circle.

STEP 2:

1. Do the same for your South Node by determining its quadrant and entering the house number and quadrant into the right circle above. This is where you are coming from and where the majority of your past life energy has been experienced. This can often be an easy area of life because you have practiced it.

2. Write two words from the description of this quadrant into the circle.

1
HOUSES 1, 2, 3
INDEPENDENCE, INDIVIDUALITY
SELF-REALIZATION, EGO,
PHYSICAL ACTIVITY

2
HOUSES 4, 5, 6
PERSONAL, PRIVATE, FAMILY,
HOME, ANCESTORS, FOOD,
NURTURING, FUN, LOVING

3
HOUSES 7, 8, 9
RELATIONSHIPS, BALANCE,
DISCERNMENT, COMMITMENT
UNDERSTANDING

4
HOUSES 10, 11, 12
CAREER, PUBLIC, SERVICE,
TECHNOLOGY, HUMANITARIAN,
SOLUTIONS, LEADERSHIP

EXERCISE
Personality Archetypes

STEP 1:

In this exercise, you will identify the two archetypes activated by each inner planet in your Natal Chart.

1. In Table 1 of your Natal Chart Navigator, look up each sign and house location for the inner planets (listed in the circles on the right of the worksheet). The key below indicates the house number and active archetype for that house.

2. Once you determine the active archetypes, write them into the appropriate circles. For instance, if you have the Sun in Aries in House 2, you would enter Warrior/Builder in the Sun circle. Please note, the Ascendant only activates an archetype by zodiac sign and not by house. Therefore, you will only write one archetype in for that circle.

House 1	Aries	The Warrior
House 2	Taurus	The Builder
House 3	Gemini	The Storyteller
House 4	Cancer	The Nurturer
House 5	Leo	The Performer
House 6	Virgo	The Craftsman
House 7	Libra	The Peacemaker
House 8	Scorpio	The Alchemist
House 9	Sagittarius	The Philosopher
House 10	Capricorn	The Entrepreneur
House 11	Aquarius	The Inventor
House 12	Pisces	The Artist

STEP 2:

Add up each of the archetypes present and list them sequentially into the blank rectangle below. This will show you which archetypes are the most powerful forces within your spirit and current personality.

> Builder (4)   Storyteller (2)
> Artist (1) Nurturer (1)
> Peacemaker (1) Entrepreneur (1)
> Philosopher (1)

STEP 3:

1. Using the example from the chapter, create a sentence describing your unique archetype blend by using the top two to create a sentence.

2. Use the remaining archetypes to generate a one- or two-word summary and insert them after your sentence in the blank circle to the right. This is a powerful way that you can connect with your internal mission for this life and embrace who you are.

ARCHETYPES

ASCENDANT
Entrepreneur

SUN
Builder
Storyteller

MOON
Builder
Storyteller

MERCURY
Builder
Nurturer

VENUS
Artist
Builder

MARS
Peacemaker
Philosopher

ARCHETYPE SUMMARY:

She is a Builder telling her Story through her Art.

Caring. Peaceful. Thoughtful. New.

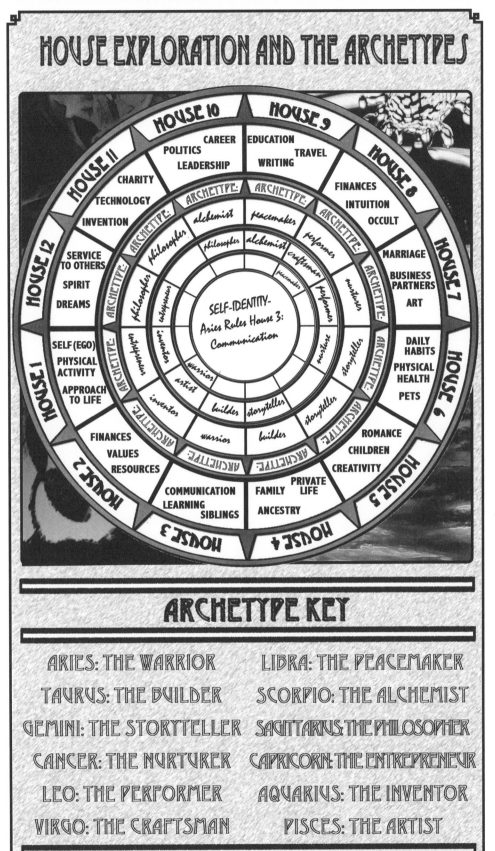

HOUSE EXPLORATION AND THE ARCHETYPES

ARCHETYPE KEY

ARIES: THE WARRIOR

TAURUS: THE BUILDER

GEMINI: THE STORYTELLER

CANCER: THE NURTURER

LEO: THE PERFORMER

VIRGO: THE CRAFTSMAN

LIBRA: THE PEACEMAKER

SCORPIO: THE ALCHEMIST

SAGITTARIUS: THE PHILOSOPHER

CAPRICORN: THE ENTREPRENEUR

AQUARIUS: THE INVENTOR

PISCES: THE ARTIST

EXERCISE
House Exploration and the Archetypes

Everyone has 12 houses in their Natal Chart, but the energy ruling over each of these houses varies based on the signs that rule them. Look to Table 2 of your Natal Chart Navigator to determine each House Ruler and Secondary Ruler in your chart as you complete the steps below.

STEP 1:

For each of the 12 houses you will write in the specific archetypes activated by the ruling signs in your chart. Using the archetype key on the House Exploration and the Archetypes worksheet, look up each sign from Table 2 and then enter this information into the appropriate house.

* Please note, there are three blank segments for each house. Write the Ruling Archetype into the outermost blank segment and then the secondary rulers into the innermost ones.

STEP 2:

You can learn a lot from this exercise, but I want to draw your attention to a specific house. The house ruled by Aries (The Warrior), represents the area of your life that will play a significant role in your development of self. For instance, if you have the House Ruler of Aries (The Warrior) in House 10, career and leadership would be integral in your path to self-actualization. On the other hand, if you have Aries (The Warrior) in House 4, your sense of self would develop primarily through your family and early home environment.

Once you find the house that is ruled by The Warrior (Aries), write that information into the inner circle.

The signs leave an energetic impression unique to you in each of the 12 Astrological Houses. Discover how they are creating their dynamic pull.

EXERCISE
Personal Life Aim

In this exercise you will determine your personal life aim through the power of your Ascendant. You will need to utilize the chart in the chapter to determine the planets that rule your chart. There will either be one or two planets based on the degree of your Ascendant. Follow the steps that follow to piece together this information.

STEP 1:

1. The first thing you will need to do to determine your life aim is to discover your personal power phrase. (You may have already circled your phrase on the worksheet!) Based on the sign of your Ascendant (see Table 1 columns 1 and 2 under Sensitive Points on your Natal Chart Navigator), look to the key to the right to determine the first portion of your personal aim.

2. Once you determine your power phrase, write it into the triangle on the Personal Life Aim worksheet at the top.

STEP 2:

1. Now you will need to utilize the chart on page 42 to determine which planets rule your chart (based on the degree of your Ascendant). Remember, if the degree is between 10–30, then you will have two planets ruling your chart.

2. Enter the planet or planets into the circles just below your personal aim.

STEP 3:

1. Now that you have determined the planets ruling your chart, it is time to find out what they mean. Based on the location of the Ruling Planet, use the zodiac sign in which it is located to determine the archetype that is helping you to fulfill your life aim.

2. Write the archetype in the circle connected to the Ruling Planet on the worksheet. If you have two Ruling Planets, make sure to write in the archetype of the other planet as well.

STEP 4:

1. To determine the area of life that the life aim is taking place in, we need to determine the house location of the Ruling Planets in your Natal Chart. Once you determine the house location use the key to determine the area of life activated.

2. Enter the area into the circle connected to the archetype. If you have two Ruling Planets, make sure to do this for both of the planets.

STEP 5:

Now it is time to finish your life aim sentence by choosing the words needed to complete it. This is an opportunity for you to draw on all of your life experiences so far to put your life aim together. Take a moment to think about all the things that have happened in your life. The events, people, and places you have experienced. Think about who you are as a personality and why you may have chosen to incarnate with these specific traits. When you're ready, complete your life aim sentence.

Personal Power Phrase

Aries: I am
Taurus: I have
Gemini: I think
Cancer: I feel
Leo: I will
Virgo: I analyze
Libra: I balance
Scorpio: I desire
Sagittarius: I aim
Capricorn: I utilize
Aquarius: I know
Pisces: I believe

Sign Archetypes

Aries: The Warrior
Taurus: The Builder
Gemini: The Storyteller
Cancer: The Nurturer
Leo: The Performer
Virgo: The Craftsman
Libra: The Peacemaker
Scorpio: The Alchemist
Sagittarius: The Philosopher
Capricorn: The Entrepreneur
Aquarius: The Inventor
Pisces: The Artist

House Areas

1: Self-development
2: Attaining Resources
3: Communication
4: Family Connection
5: Creative/Playful
6: Service/Efficiency
7: Partnership
8: Spiritual Rebirth
9: Written Word/Philosophy
10: Career/Leadership
11: Humanitarian
12: Spiritual Belief/Art

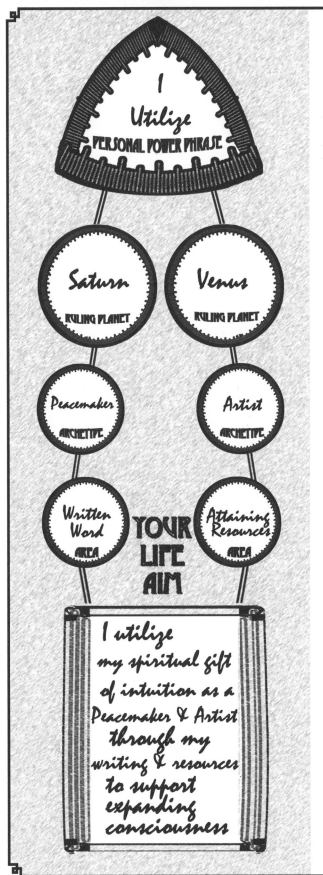

Guided Fill in the Blank Life Aim Directions

Now it is time to finish your life aim sentence by choosing the words needed to complete it. These phrases are to be created by you. There is no right or wrong. Use your imagination. This is an opportunity for you to draw on all of your life experiences so far to put your life aim together. Take a moment to think about all the things that have happened in your life. The events, people, and places you have experienced. Think about who you are as a personality and why you may have chosen to incarnate with these specific traits.

STEP 1:

1. To get started you will transfer the information you just completed in the column to the left onto the blank lines below. Following the three prompts below write the specific information on to the first blank line labeled one.

2. You will now fill out the second blank line labeled two by creating your own phrases. The purpose of these phrases is to connect the information together to create a life aim sentence. Before you get started, take a moment to digest the information you have already entered onto the first line. Once you are ready, create your own phrase on the second line that will connect the pieces of information to create a sentence.

PROMPT 1:
Enter Personal Power Phrase on line 1 (see top triangle to the left)

1. *I utilize*

2. *my spiritual gift of intuition as a*

PROMPT 2:
Enter Archetypes on line 1 (see middle circles to the left)

1. *Peacemaker & Artist*

2. *through my*

PROMPT 3:
Enter Areas on line 1 (see bottom circles to the left):

1. *writing & resources*

2. *to support expanding consciousness*

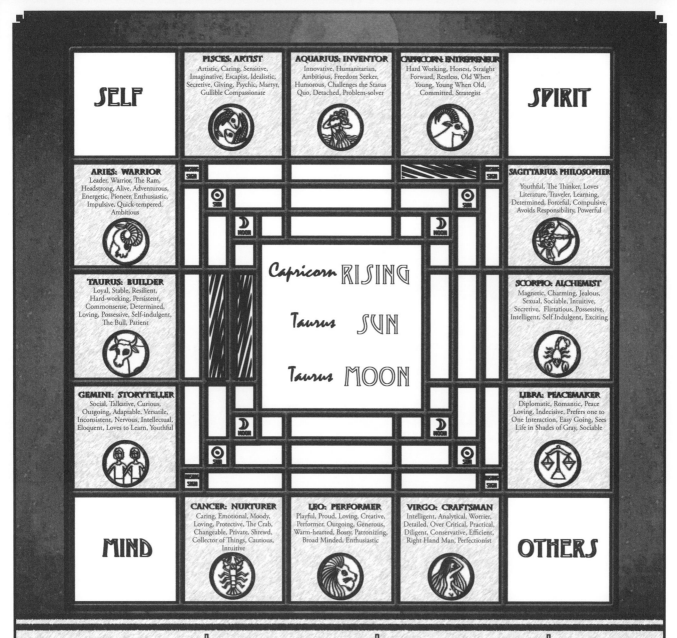

SELF

PISCES: ARTIST
Artistic, Caring, Sensitive, Imaginative, Escapist, Idealistic, Secretive, Giving, Psychic, Martyr, Gullible Compassionate

AQUARIUS: INVENTOR
Innovative, Humanitarian, Ambitious, Freedom Seeker, Humorous, Challenges the Status Quo, Detached, Problem-solver

CAPRICORN: ENTREPRENEUR
Hard Working, Honest, Straight Forward, Restless, Old When Young, Young When Old, Committed, Strategist

SPIRIT

ARIES: WARRIOR
Leader, Warrior, The Ram, Headstrong, Alive, Adventurous, Energetic, Pioneer, Enthusiastic, Impulsive, Quick-tempered, Ambitious

SAGITTARIUS: PHILOSOPHER
Youthful, The Thinker, Loves Literature, Traveler, Learning, Determined, Forceful, Compulsive, Avoids Responsibility, Powerful

TAURUS: BUILDER
Loyal, Stable, Resilient, Hard-working, Persistent, Commonsense, Determined, Loving, Possessive, Self-indulgent, The Bull, Patient

SCORPIO: ALCHEMIST
Magnetic, Charming, Jealous, Sexual, Sociable, Intuitive, Secretive, Flirtatious, Possessive, Intelligent, Self Indulgent, Exciting

Capricorn RISING

Taurus SUN

Taurus MOON

GEMINI: STORYTELLER
Social, Talkative, Curious, Outgoing, Adaptable, Versatile, Inconsistent, Nervous, Intellectual, Eloquent, Loves to Learn, Youthful

LIBRA: PEACEMAKER
Diplomatic, Romantic, Peace Loving, Indecisive, Prefers one to One Interaction, Easy Going, Sees Life in Shades of Gray, Sociable

MIND

CANCER: NURTURER
Caring, Emotional, Moody, Loving, Protective, The Crab, Changeable, Private, Shrewd, Collector of Things, Cautious, Intuitive

LEO: PERFORMER
Playful, Proud, Loving, Creative, Performer, Outgoing, Generous, Warm-hearted, Bossy, Patronizing, Broad Minded, Enthusiastic

VIRGO: CRAFTSMAN
Intelligent, Analytical, Worrier, Detailed, Over Critical, Practical, Diligent, Conservative, Efficient, Right Hand Man, Perfectionist

OTHERS

EXERCISE
Personal Profile

In this exercise we will be exploring the energies that make up your Astrological Name. These three powerful forces represent the spiritual recipe that offers you insight into how individuals outside your inner circle are experiencing your personality. Each of the outer squares represents a zodiac sign and the adjectives that describe how that energy can be interpreted. Each of the blank inner boxes correspond with the Rising Sign, Sun sign, and Moon sign (look in the corner squares to identify which one). Follow the steps that follow to reveal what it is that others are seeing.

STEP 1:

1. Enter your Astrological Name into the inner square above by filling in the blanks, i.e.,Taurus Rising, Pisces Sun, Libra Moon by using the Natal Chart Navigator columns 1 and 2.

2. Now that you have identified the zodiac sign for your Rising Sign, Sun, and Moon look to the inner blank boxes. Shade the box for the zodiac sign activated. For example, the three boxes to the right of the square labeled Taurus are associated with Taurus.

STEP 2:

1. Each of these signs has words and adjectives to describe how these energies can be expressed. Remember, we are exploring these power players to gain insight into the cliff notes version of yourself. Read through all of the adjectives. Select three from each sign that you feel are the most accurate and write them in the space at the bottom right of your worksheet.

2. Now begin to meditate on the impact this has on those you meet.

STEP 3:

Honest
Stable Loyal
Loving
Straightforward
Entreprenew
Determined

Resilient

Self-indulgent

THE INFLUENCES OF THE OUTER PLANETS

JUPITER

LUCK & GOOD
FORTUNE

Philosopher

*Travel, Education
& Writing*

SATURN

LIFE LESSONS
TO BE LEARNED

Philosopher

*Travel, Education
& Writing*

URANUS

WHERE THE UNUSUAL
OR UNEXPECTED
OCCURS

Inventor

*Your people &
Love given*

NEPTUNE

DIFFICULTY SEEING
THINGS AS THEY
TRULY ARE

Artist

*Mental & Spiritual
Health*

PLUTO

WHERE THE MOST
SPIRITUAL GROWTH
OCCURS

Philosopher

*Travel, Education
& Writing*

EXERCISE
The Influences of the Outer Planets

In this exercise, you will begin to explore how the outer planets are influencing your life. Each house is numbered on the worksheet The Influences of the Outer Planets. The area of life affected by each house is listed on the outermost portion of the circle. The archetype activated by house is listed on the inside of the circle. This exercise is designed to give you a brief overview of how these planets can be interpreted in your Natal Chart. Be sure to read more about the houses in the chapter to find out even more!

STEP 1:

Using your Natal Chart information, look to see where the social planets (Jupiter and Saturn) are located in your chart. Because these planets have a direct impact on your internal world, enter them into the inner portion of the circle on the worksheet.

STEP 2:

Based on the location of Jupiter and Saturn, fill in the activated archetype and area of life (found in the rings of the circle) into the boxes below to discover what each of these planets is telling you in your Natal Chart.

STEP 3:

Now it is time to explore the remaining outer planets. Look to see where Uranus, Neptune, and Pluto are located in your Natal Chart. Enter their locations into the outermost portion of the circle to the left.

STEP 4:

Based on the location of Uranus, Neptune, and Pluto, fill in the activated archetype and area of life (found in the rings of the circle) into the boxes below to discover what each of the planets is telling you in your Natal Chart.

EXERCISE
The Fortunes

In this exercise we will finally be able to put all of the pieces of the puzzle together. We will journey back through the information we discovered in previous exercises to gain full clarity. We will see how all that was revealed to us through our Natal Chart fits together.

STEP 1:

1. Looking back to chapter 3 and the Divine Life Purpose: Uncovering the Mystery of your Moon Nodes worksheet, enter your South and North Moon Nodes into the circle on The Fortunes worksheet.

2. Draw an arrow from the South Moon Node to the North Node to indicate the direction of this current incarnation.

STEP 2:

Looking back to chapter 5, enter your specific life aim into the middle of the circle.

STEP 3:

1. Using the information on your Natal Chart Navigator, determine the house that your Part of Fortune is located in.

2. Write your Part of Fortune into the big circle on the worksheet.

3. Look to see the house and archetype activated by its location to determine what you "want" in this life.

4. Once you specify this "want" write it into the box below the circle.

STEP 4:

1. You should have a firm understanding of the spiritual direction you anticipated for this current incarnation. We will now look to see how you are going to achieve this. To determine the amount of fate and free will that you are working with, look back to chapter 2.

2. Enter the number of planets from the left side of your chart into the Free Will box.

3. Enter the number of planets on the right side of your chart into the Fate box.

STEP 5:

1. To understand the gifts you chose prior to this incarnation to assist you in achieving this goal, look to the Elements and Modes worksheet in chapter 1 to determine the most dominant element and mode in your chart.

2. Check the circle or triangle that applies. If there was a tie, check both. The gift of that element and mode is noted below the circles.

STEP 6:

Now we will determine the aspects of your personality that you chose prior to incarnating to support you on your path. Looking back to chapter 4, enter the three most dominant archetypes from your personality to discover your greatest gifts.

Now claim your power.

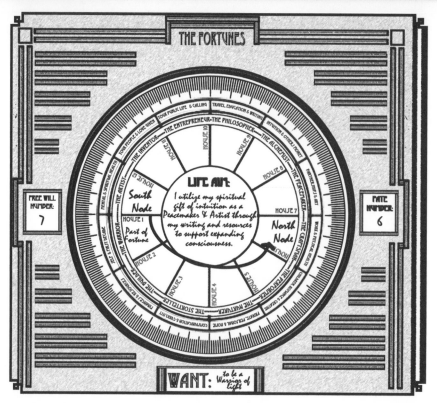

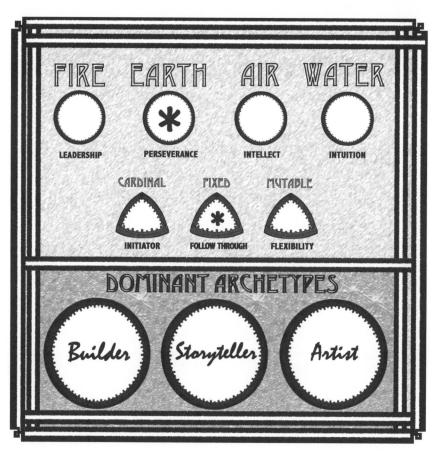

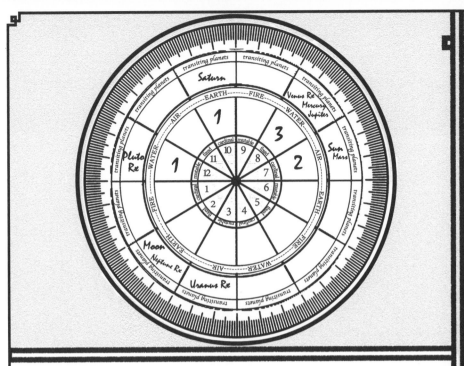

FIRE: 0
spiritual, birthing, beginnings, leadership, confidence, ego development, aggression, physical movement.

EARTH: 3
securing resources, grounding, efficiency, livelihood, finances, career, roots, stability, home.

AIR: 3
learning, communication, socializing, new activities, broad perspective, debating, philosophizing.

WATER: 4
emotional, connection, intuitive, breaking through limitations, time for releasing emotional pain.

◦MODE◦

CARDINAL: 3
this is a time for action.

FIXED: 5
this is a time for persistence.

MUTABLE: 2
this is a time to bend with the wind.

◦FORECAST◦

◦ELEMENT◦
WATER
Connection,
Breaking through limitations,
emotional
◦MODE◦

this is a time for
PERSISTENCE!

EXERCISE
Aligning with the Cycles

STEP 1:

In Table 3 of your Natal Chart Navigator, you will be able to determine the house that each planet is currently transiting in your chart. On the blank outermost portion of the circle on the Aligning with the Cycles worksheet, write each of the transiting planets' location into the appropriate houses. If a planet is currently retrograde, it will be noted next to the planet name in Table 3. If the planet is retrograde, write "Rx" next to its name. Use the key below to help you keep track of the planets you've marked.

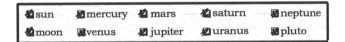

☑ sun   ☑ mercury   ☑ mars   ☑ saturn   ☑ neptune

☑ moon   ☐ venus   ☑ jupiter   ☑ uranus   ☑ pluto

STEP 2:

1. Add up the total number of planets in each house.

2. Write this number into the blank inner segment circle. Notice the element and mode activated in each house as you enter the number.

STEP 3:

Each house, just like each zodiac sign, is represented by an element and mode. For each of the 12 houses, the element and mode have been written into the worksheet. Each of the elements and a short description is written in the column to the right of the circle on the worksheet.

1. Add the total numbers for each element: Fire, Earth, Air, and Water and write them next to the element name in the right hand column.

2. Also do this for the modes: Cardinal, Fixed, and Mutable.

STEP 4:

By determining the element and mode that are most dominant, you will be able to decipher the current "weather" forecast for your life.

1. Pick three words from the most dominant element definition and enter them into the "Forecast" portion to the right.

2. Just below that, you will enter the phrase associated with your most dominant mode. If there is a tie between two elements or modes, write both down in the "Forecast."

As we continue to discover how the forces of the unseen are influencing your life, keep these insights in mind.

EXERCISE
Taking Flight with Saturn

There are four distinct phases that Saturn moves through in one cycle (29.5 years). We spend roughly 7.5 years in each phase of this cycle. These four phases correspond to the four quadrants of the Natal Chart and are labeled appropriately on this worksheet.

STEP 1:
1. When you were born, Saturn was located in one of these four quadrants/phases based on its location in the houses. In Table 1 of your Natal Chart Navigator, locate the house that Saturn was located in at the moment of your birth.

2. Using the blank inner segments of the circle, write "Natal Saturn" into the appropriate house.

STEP 2:
To determine the house Saturn currently is in, look to Table 3 of your Natal Chart Navigator. Once you determine Saturn's current location in the houses, write "Transiting Saturn" into the appropriate house of the outermost blank segment of the circle.

STEP 3:
1. We will now determine the phase Saturn was in when you were born. Look to see the quadrant and phase activated by Natal Saturn (it's written in each quadrant). Enter this phase into the first blank circle at the bottom left of the worksheet.

2. To the left bottom of the worksheet, the phases have been broken down and key words selected. Pick one key word and write it within this circle.

STEP 4:
1. We will now determine which phase Transiting Saturn activates. Determine the active phase and then enter it into the blank circle at the bottom.

2. To the left bottom of the worksheet, the phases have been broken down and key words selected. Pick one key word and write it within this circle.

* To determine your gateways, read the block entitled Navigating with Saturn—Extra!

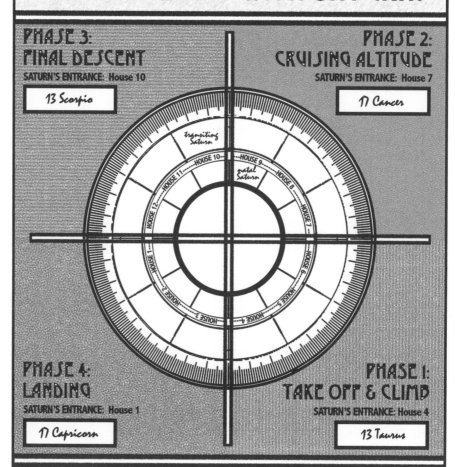

TAKING FLIGHT WITH SATURN!

PHASE 3:
FINAL DESCENT
SATURN'S ENTRANCE: House 10

13 Scorpio

PHASE 2:
CRUISING ALTITUDE
SATURN'S ENTRANCE: House 7

17 Cancer

PHASE 4:
LANDING
SATURN'S ENTRANCE: House 1

17 Capricorn

PHASE 1:
TAKE OFF & CLIMB
SATURN'S ENTRANCE: House 4

13 Taurus

PHASE 1: TAKE OFF & CLIMB
new beginnings, career opportunity, relocation, sense of moving forward, your life begins anew

PHASE 2: CRUISING ALTITUDE
promotion, advancement, progress, sense of covering ground, all action resulting in a culminating event

PHASE 3: FINAL DESCENT
preparation, a need to put things in order, a slight slowing down, a very purposeful time period

PHASE 4: LANDING
holding/waiting period, internal reflection, reaping the karma of past actions in this life started in phases 1 &2

NAVIGATING WITH SATURN - EXTRA!

Saturn is always moving through the zodiac. There are four points on its journey that are unique to you and mark the changing of the phases in your life. To determine these critical junctures, we can mark the four gateways in the chart above.

The 4 pivotal turning points (gateways) are dependent on the starting points of your 1st, 4th, 7th and 10th house. Using Table 2 of your Natal Chart Navigator, you will determine the zodiac sign and degree for the pivotal House Rulers. There is a box in each quadrant where you can enter this information. Pay attention as Saturn moves through the zodiac and through the signs: Aries, Taurus, Gemini, Cancer, Leo, Virgo, Libra, Scorpio, Sagittarius, Capricorn, Aquarius and Pisces When it hits the degree notated for your specific chart and gateways, you will have begun a new phase of the Saturn transit. You can use this information to time important events and gain valuable insight into how your life will unfold. To view the current planetary positions, visit:

www.absolutelyastrology.com

I ENTERED THE SATURN CYCLE IN THE PHASE:

I'M CURRENTLY IN THIS PHASE:

CURRENT IMPACT: *House 8 - Opportunity to deepen connection to spirit*   **COMING UP:** *House 9 - Discovering life purpose - Power Illumination Period*

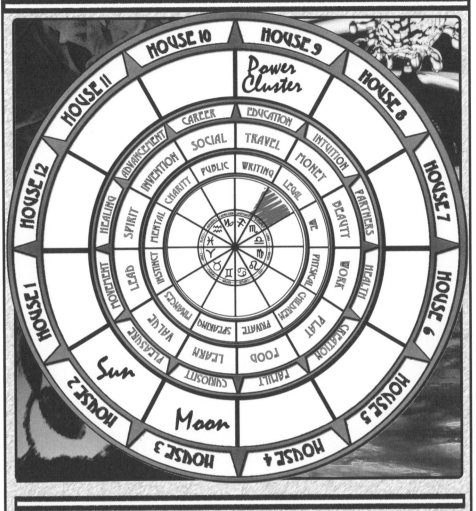

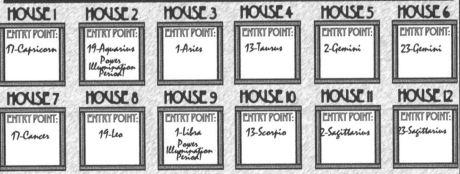

HOUSE 1	HOUSE 2	HOUSE 3	HOUSE 4	HOUSE 5	HOUSE 6
ENTRY POINT: 17-Capricorn	**ENTRY POINT:** 19-Aquarius *Power Illumination Period!*	**ENTRY POINT:** 1-Aries	**ENTRY POINT:** 13-Taurus	**ENTRY POINT:** 2-Gemini	**ENTRY POINT:** 23-Gemini

HOUSE 7	HOUSE 8	HOUSE 9	HOUSE 10	HOUSE 11	HOUSE 12
ENTRY POINT: 17-Cancer	**ENTRY POINT:** 19-Leo	**ENTRY POINT:** 1-Libra *Power Illumination Period!*	**ENTRY POINT:** 13-Scorpio	**ENTRY POINT:** 2-Sagittarius	**ENTRY POINT:** 23-Sagittarius

EXTRA—KEEPING TRACK OF JUPITER

You can easily align with the gifts of Jupiter by watching it journey through your chart! To determine when Jupiter will enter a new house, we will add the house Entry Points into the boxes above. Looking to Table 2 of your Natal Chart Navigator, enter the sign and degree of your House Ruler into the squares. When Jupiter is at those specific degrees, it is entering a new house in your chart and illuminating that area of your life.

You can keep track of the current location of Jupiter at www.absolutelyastrology.com.

In this exercise, you determined the location of your Sun, Moon, and Power Clusters. This information indicates a Power Illumination Period. Add "Power Illumination Period" into the squares to keep track of when Jupiter will enter those periods! Time your actions for heightened results!

STEP 1:

Before exploring the impact of Transiting Jupiter, we first must determine our Power Illumination Periods. We do this by entering our Natal Sun, Natal Moon, and relevant Power Clusters on to the worksheet. Looking to Table 1 of your Natal Chart Navigator, determine the house location for your Natal Sun and Natal Moon. Enter their location into the outermost blank portion of the Natal Chart circle.

STEP 2:

We originally explored Power Clusters (3 or more planets in a house) in chapter 1. Looking back to the second exercise for that chapter, determine if you identified a Power Cluster in your chart. If one was present, add "Power Cluster" to the outermost circle and appropriate house.

STEP 3:

Using Table 3 of your Natal Chart Navigator, determine the house that Jupiter is currently transiting in your chart. Once this is determined, shade in the innermost blank segment of the Natal Chart that corresponds to that house. Remember, if you shaded a house that also has the Sun, Moon, or Power Cluster, you are currently in a Power Illumination Period.

STEP 4:

1. In this chapter there is a detailed description of Jupiter's impact in each house. Looking back in the chapter, locate the house that Jupiter is currently transiting in your chart.

2. Based on your reflection of this information, write a sentence on its impact next to "Current Impact" (at the top of the worksheet beneath the title). Note, if Jupiter is transiting a house of a Power Illumination Period, add "Power Illumination Period."

STEP 5:

1. It's time to determine what Jupiter has in store for you next! Jupiter moves through the houses numerically: if it is currently in House 9, it will be moving to House 10 next. Look back in the chapter to read more about the house Jupiter will transit next.

2. Write one sentence next to the "Coming Up" section (at the bottom of this exercise). Note, if Jupiter will be transiting a house of a Power Illumination Period, add "Power Illumination Period."

COMPATIBILITY REPORT:

I am most compatible with another when their Rising Sign/Ascendant is in the same Element as my own.

The element of my Rising Sign is:

__EARTH__

The three signs of this element are:

1. Capricorn
2. Taurus
3. Virgo

To determine if there is an additional harmonic indication, we can look to see if an aspect has been formed. When Rising Sign's are in the same element, there are only two aspects that can be formed: the trine (120-degrees apart) and the conjunction (0-degrees apart). Follow instructions in Exercise - Part 1, enter your allowable orb here:

__5__ -- __19__

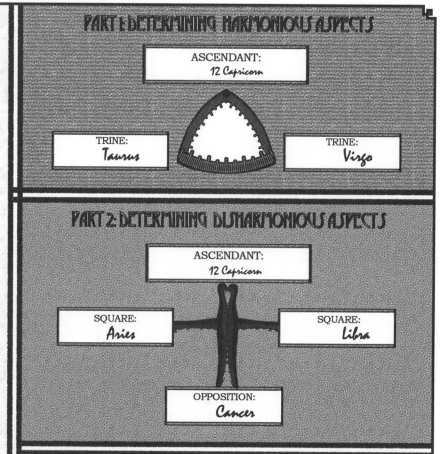

⊙ My sun is in the sign: Taurus

....if their Moon is in this same sign, this is a strong indication of harmony.

My Moon is in the sign: Taurus ☽

....if their Sun is in this same sign, this is a strong indication of harmony.

Without other harmonious indications, those whose Ascendant squares or oppose my Ascendant, will most likely result in a disharmonious relationship. These three signs are:

1. Aries (square)
2. Cancer (opposition)
3. Libra (square)

PART 1: DETERMINING HARMONIOUS ASPECTS

ASCENDANT:
12 Capricorn

TRINE:
Taurus

TRINE:
Virgo

PART 2: DETERMINING DISHARMONIOUS ASPECTS

ASCENDANT:
12 Capricorn

SQUARE:
Aries

SQUARE:
Libra

OPPOSITION:
Cancer

HARMONIOUS ASPECTS

TRINE: HARMONIOUS ASPECT
(120-degrees apart)
Harmonious relationship due to the activation of the same element. Below lists the signs that trine each other.

FIRE:

| Aries | Leo | Sagittarius |

EARTH:

| Taurus | Virgo | Capricorn |

AIR:

| Gemini | Libra | Aquarius |

WATER:

| Cancer | Scorpio | Pisces |

CONJUNCTION: HARMONIOUS ASPECT
(0-degrees apart)
Harmonious relationship due to the activation of the same Element and Mode. This means that they are in the exact same sign. If they are within 7-degrees of each other, then the aspect is heightened.

DISHARMONIOUS ASPECTS

OPPOSITION: DISHARMONIOUS ASPECT
(180-degrees apart)
Signs that appear across from one another in the zodiac are in opposition.

Aries - Libra
Taurus - Scorpio
Gemini - Sagittarius
Cancer - Capricorn
Leo - Aquarius
Virgo - Pisces

SQUARE: DISHARMONIOUS ASPECT
(90-degrees apart)
Disharmonious relationship due to the activation of the same mode, but being in different elements. Below lists each sign and the two signs that square it.

Aries: Cancer & Capricorn
Taurus: Leo & Aquarius
Gemini: Virgo & Pisces
Cancer: Libra & Aries
Leo: Scorpio & Taurus
Virgo: Sagittarius & Gemini
Libra: Capricorn & Cancer
Scorpio: Aquarius & Leo
Sagittarius: Pisces & Virgo
Capricorn: Aries & Libra
Aquarius: Taurus & Scorpio
Pisces: Gemini & Sagittarius

Relationship Compatibility through the Aspects

There are four primary aspects that can be made between planets/sensitive points. Two are considered harmonious: the trine and the conjunction. Two are considered disharmonious: the square and the opposition. When looking to see how you will interact with a companion, business partner, employee, or friend, you can compare your charts to determine how harmonious or disharmonious the union may be. Please note, disharmonious aspects are not necessarily an indication that you should immediately abandon the relationship. They merely indicate that there will be more "kinks" to work out along the way.

PART 1—DIRECTIONS

STEP 1:
The strongest indicator for whether or not a relationship will be harmonious can be determined by comparing the position of the Ascendant/Rising Sign. Just as certain musical notes blend well, others do not. Your Rising Sign will interact with each of the 12 signs in specific ways. Because of this ability to determine if planets will harmonize or not, Astrology can be utilized to predict how two individuals would most likely function in a relationship.

Use the information in Table 1 of your Natal Chart Navigator to enter the sign and degree of your Ascendant into the worksheet Part 1.

* Remember the Ascendant/Rising Sign are being compared, not the Sun Signs.

STEP 2:
Rising Signs that share the same element will naturally be more compatible with one another. This is because they approach life in a similar fashion, and they will naturally harmonize through their behaviors, goals, and values. In the Harmonious Aspects Key in the shaded lower left middle section of the worksheet, the signs have been sorted by element for you.

1.   When you locate your sign and element, add the remaining two signs into the worksheet, Part 1.

2.   Go ahead and enter the element of your Rising Sign and the three signs you recorded into the Compatibility Report.

STEP 3:
This harmonious indication (determined when elements are the same) can be heightened. If the Rising Signs are in aspect to one another, this serves as further validation to the harmonic indication. There are only two aspects that can be formed when in the same element: the Conjunction (0-degrees apart) and the Trine (120-degrees apart). Remember, the aspect does not need to be exact to be significant. This is why we need to determine what the allowable orb is for your chart.

1.   Look to the worksheet in Part 1 to see the degree you entered for your Rising Sign, then both add and subtract 7-degrees from this number to determine the allowable orb.

2.   Please add this information to the Compatibility Report.

* Note, if the Rising Sign of another is in this allowable orb, an aspect has been made. If it is in the same sign, a conjunction is formed. If it is one of the other two signs, a trine has been formed.

STEP 4:
The other strong indication of a harmonious relationship occurs if your Sun is located in the same sign as their Moon or if your Moon is located in the same sign as their Sun. Using Table 1 in your Natal Chart Navigator, add this information to the Compatibility Report accordingly.

*Note: If the Moons are in the same sign, this is also a harmonious indication.

PART 2—DIRECTIONS

STEP 1:
There are three Rising Signs that you will naturally struggle to harmonize with. These three signs consist of the two signs that Square your Ascendant/Rising Sign and the sign that opposes it.

To determine the disharmonious signs, enter your Ascendant/Rising Sign and degree into the worksheet, Part 2.

STEP 2:
To determine the sign that opposes your Ascendant, look to the lower portion of the Disharmonious Aspects Key in the shaded area at the lower middle left on the worksheet: there will be six pairs of signs that are in opposition. When you locate your sign within one of these pairs, the other sign that it is paired with represents the sign that it opposes. Enter this sign into the box for "Opposition" in the worksheet, Part 2. This sign is naturally 180 degrees apart from your Rising Sign and appears on the opposite side of the zodiac.

* Note, this is a particularly curious combination and can often indicate a relationship that comes on strong, but does not withstand the test of time. This is due to the complementary element and same mode as discussed in the chapter.

STEP 3:
The next step is to determine the two signs that square your Ascendant. In the upper portion of the Disharmonious Aspect Key, there is a list of all 12 signs and the two signs that square them. Locate the sign of your Ascendant/Rising Sign and then enter the two signs into the boxes in the worksheet, Part 2. If an individual has their Ascendant in one of these two signs, the relationship will most likely be disharmonious. Just like oil separates from water, there are some combinations of energies that simply do not harmonize well. This is not to the fault of any one type of individual, but rather to the inherent nature involved with the differing approaches, tendencies, and traits we bring into each incarnation.

STEP 4:
Enter these three signs into the Compatibility Report and note if they are a "square" or "opposition." The orb that you previously calculated applies here as well. If an individual has a Rising Sign that is in aspect by square or opposition, this is an especially heightened indication that the relationship will be disharmonious. Remember, there are fated relationships and those we enter into by choice. If you discover you are in a relationship that is not harmonious, do not panic! If the relationship was fated (mother, father, child) there is a hidden karmic gift. Release your need to control their approach to life, accept that it is appropriate for the development of their spirit in this life. Harmonize on the areas that you can and let everything else go...

* Note: It is worth looking at the location of the Sun and Moon in both charts even if there is a disharmonious relationship between the Ascendants. A good aspect there could help counteract the trouble that would come about if an individual's Ascendant were in one of these three signs.

EXERCISE
Life Lessons

Each of us are students in this "spiritual school." Through the lessons and curriculum of our earthly experience, we will master various lessons until we ascend to a higher plane of existence. The Natal Chart offers valuable information on these lessons and can highlight if any of them are of particular importance in your life.

STEP 1:
Using Table 1 of your Natal Chart Navigator, determine the sign each planet was located in at the moment of your birth. Enter the sign next to the list of planets in the Natal Planet Location to the right.

STEP 2:
Now that you have entered the location of your planets, we need to determine if any of them were located in a heightened position. To the right of the planet list, there are four columns that list the heightened positions for that planet. If the sign you entered matches any of these signs listed, circle the name of the sign in the column.

STEP 3:
Each of the columns (A,B,C & D) represent the four heightened positions a planet can take in the zodiac. If you circled one of these positions, this is a very important lesson for you in this life. The first two columns (A & B) represent Rulership and Exaltation. The last two columns (C & D) represent Detriment and Fall. Looking back to see which planets were in heightened locations, write the name of the planet into the appropriate circles to the right. Remember, Column A & B represent Rulership and Exaltation. Column C & D represent Determine and Fall.

STEP 4:
You have now identified which planets were in heightened locations. Planets that are in Rulership or Exaltation represent lessons you have mastered and indicate areas of your life where you will experience ease. Planets in Detriment or Fall represent lessons you are working on and require your attention. These lessons may be a point of frustration in your life and you must be patient with yourself. The next step is to identify the lessons of each of these planets specifically. In the key below, determine the specific lesson of the planet and enter it below the appropriate circle under "Mastered Lessons" or "New Lessons."

STEP 5:
Take a moment to meditate on what you've discovered. Be thankful for the opportunity to be aware of your past life and progress—know at your core, what is new versus mastered.

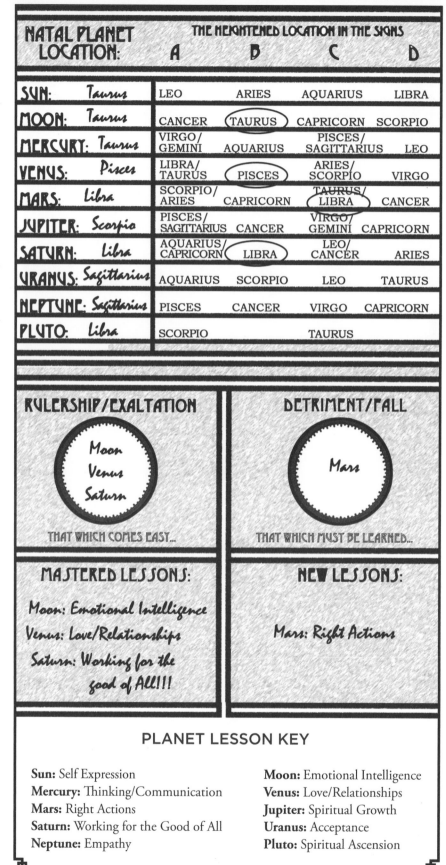

NATAL PLANET LOCATION:		THE HEIGHTENED LOCATION IN THE SIGNS			
		A	**B**	**C**	**D**
SUN:	Taurus	LEO	ARIES	AQUARIUS	LIBRA
MOON:	Taurus	CANCER	(TAURUS)	CAPRICORN	SCORPIO
MERCURY:	Taurus	VIRGO/GEMINI	AQUARIUS	PISCES/SAGITTARIUS	LEO
VENUS:	Pisces	LIBRA/TAURUS	(PISCES)	ARIES/SCORPIO	VIRGO
MARS:	Libra	SCORPIO/ARIES	CAPRICORN	TAURUS/(LIBRA)	CANCER
JUPITER:	Scorpio	PISCES/SAGITTARIUS	CANCER	VIRGO/GEMINI	CAPRICORN
SATURN:	Libra	AQUARIUS/CAPRICORN	(LIBRA)	LEO/CANCER	ARIES
URANUS:	Sagittarius	AQUARIUS	SCORPIO	LEO	TAURUS
NEPTUNE:	Sagittarius	PISCES	CANCER	VIRGO	CAPRICORN
PLUTO:	Libra	SCORPIO		TAURUS	

RULERSHIP/EXALTATION

Moon
Venus
Saturn

THAT WHICH COMES EASY...

DETRIMENT/FALL

Mars

THAT WHICH MUST BE LEARNED...

MASTERED LESSONS:

Moon: Emotional Intelligence
Venus: Love/Relationships
Saturn: Working for the good of ALL!!!

NEW LESSONS:

Mars: Right Actions

PLANET LESSON KEY

Sun: Self Expression
Mercury: Thinking/Communication
Mars: Right Actions
Saturn: Working for the Good of All
Neptune: Empathy

Moon: Emotional Intelligence
Venus: Love/Relationships
Jupiter: Spiritual Growth
Uranus: Acceptance
Pluto: Spiritual Ascension

In this exercise we will begin to explore the dynamic power the Moon holds over the success you have in accomplishing your goals. Before completing this exercise, you will need to gain access to a Moon Phase calendar. Please visit www.absolutelyastrology.com to view the current and upcoming phases of the Moon. This exercise can be repeated as many times as you would like, so if you're anticipating using it multiple times, please photocopy prior to completing.

STEP 1:

Regardless of what phase the Moon is in at the time you are completing this exercise, you are absolutely capable of immediately aligning with its energetic pull.

In the circles labeled Goal 1, 2 & 3 on the left bottom of the Moon Planner worksheet, fill in 3 goals or activities that you would like to accomplish in the next 30 days. Choose anything that is relevant in your life currently. There is no action too small or too big for aligning with the power of the Moon.

STEP 2:

There are two specific energetic patterns present through the cyclical nature of the Moon: the waning phases (Full Moon to New Moon) and the waxing phases (New Moon to Full Moon). The charts on the right of the worksheet will explain the dynamics present and the possible activities that will likely have a beneficial outcome when performed during those specific phases. The success you have in achieving the goals you created depends on numerous factors, but the energy of the Moon can either support or hinder the success of these goals.

1. Based on the table and examples to the right, determine whether the goal you are trying to achieve is best suited for either the waxing or waning phases of the Moon.
2. Enter either waning or waxing in the box connected to the specific goal you are analyzing.

STEP 3:

Once you determine the Moon Phase that is most appropriate for your goal/activity, look to the Moon Phase calendar to pick the date that you will either begin or complete the activity listed.

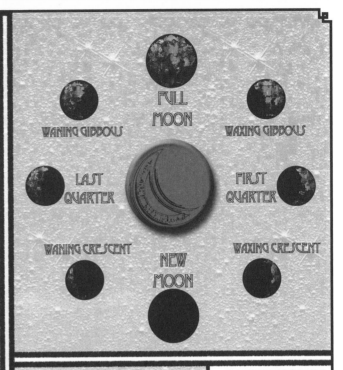

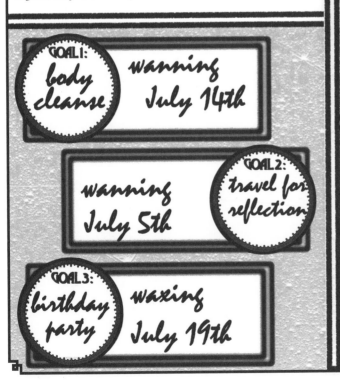

NEW MOON - FULL MOON (WAXING PHASES)

THE WAXING PHASES OF THE MOON ARE AN EXTERNAL AND EXTROVERTED TIME. THIS IS WHEN YOU WILL BE REWARDED FOR SOCIAL ENDEAVORS AND STARTING NEW PROJECTS THAT CAN PROPEL YOUR LIFE FORWARD. THIS IS A TIME PERIOD WHERE IT IS EASIEST TO ADD ON NEW AND FUN ENERGY TO YOUR LIFE.

START A NEW PROJECT
BEGIN A NEW STUDY
GO SHOPPING
TRAVEL FOR PLEASURE
START A NEW JOB
BUY SOMETHING NEW
TRAIN SOMEONE
BEGIN A SAVINGS ACCT
THROW A PARTY
FIX SOMETHING
DIET - TO GAIN WEIGHT
COLLECT A DEBT
BEAUTY TREATMENT

BREAK A BAD HABIT
TRAVEL FOR REFLECTION
DIET - TO LOSE WEIGHT
CANNING OF FOOD
PLANT SEEDS
READ A BOOK
MEDITATION
BORROW MONEY
START THERAPY
GET A MASSAGE
START A CLEANSE
CLEAN YOUR HOUSE

FULL MOON - NEW MOON (WANING PHASES)

THE WANING PHASES OF THE MOON ARE A TIME FOR REFLECTION AND ARE HIGHLY INTROVERTED. THIS IS A TIME TO RELEASE AND LET GO OF THAT WHICH NO LONGER SERVES YOU. ANYTHING THAT YOU WOULD LIKE TO SAY GOODBYE TO OR RELEASE BACK TO THE WORLD CAN BEST BE DONE NOW.

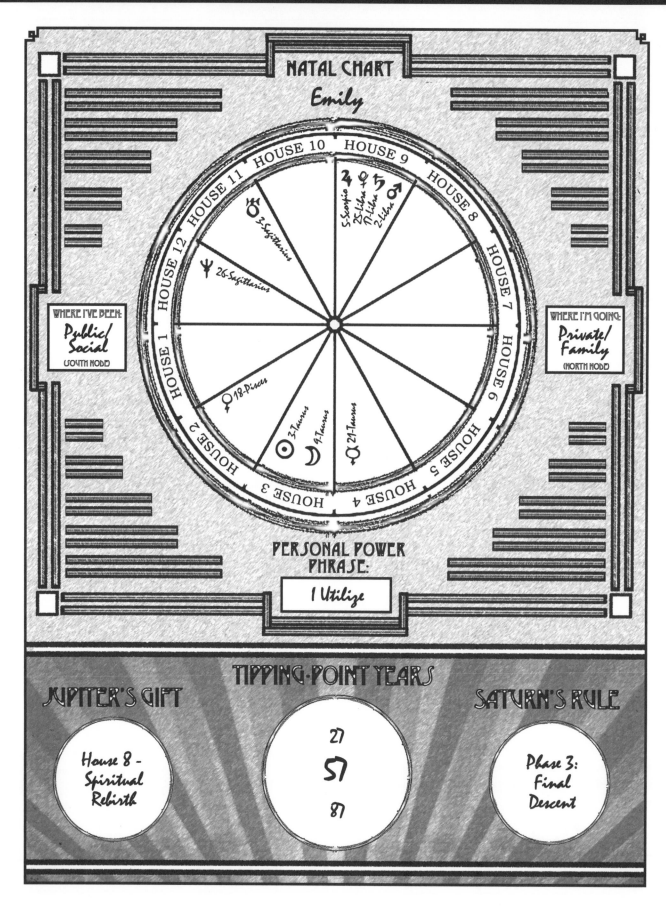

NATAL CHART

Emily

HOUSE 10 · HOUSE 9 · HOUSE 11 · HOUSE 8 · HOUSE 12 · HOUSE 7 · HOUSE 1 · HOUSE 6 · HOUSE 2 · HOUSE 5 · HOUSE 3 · HOUSE 4

3-Sagittarius

26-Sagittarius

5-Scorpio
25-Libra + ♀
7-Libra
2-Libra

18-Pisces

3-Taurus
9-Taurus
21-Taurus

WHERE I'VE BEEN:
Public/ Social
(SOUTH NODE)

WHERE I'M GOING:
Private/ Family
(NORTH NODE)

PERSONAL POWER PHRASE:

I Utilize

TIPPING-POINT YEARS

JUPITER'S GIFT

House 8 - Spiritual Rebirth

27
57
87

SATURN'S RULE

Phase 3: Final Descent

EXERCISE
Completing Your Natal Chart

It's now time to put together all of the insights you have discovered through this spiritual journey in your official Natal Chart. May it serve as deep validation and inspiration to your spirit.

Start by writing your name just below the words "Natal Chart" on the worksheet.

STEP 1:

1. The most important thing to remember as you move forward is the spiritual direction of your life. For that information, we look to the Moon Nodes and the insights we discovered in chapter 3. Looking back to that exercise, determine the quadrants where your South and North Node are located. In the Moon Node Mode key at the bottom boxes of the worksheet, a key word has been selected for each quadrant. In the box on the left side of your Natal Chart; enter the key word for the quadrant for where you've been (South Node).

2. In the box on the right side of your Natal Chart, enter the key word for where you're going (North Node).

STEP 2:

Every person has a personal power phrase that ignites the flame of their soul's purpose. In chapter 5, you discovered your personal power phrase based on your Rising Sign. There is a key of these personal power phrases in the bottom left box of the worksheet. Enter your personal power phrase into the box below your Natal Chart.

STEP 3:

It's now time to enter the location of each planet at the moment of your birth. This part of the exercise can be done in any way that specifically inspires YOU. The symbols for the signs and planets are located in the keys in the bottom right boxes of the worksheet. You can choose to use some of the symbols or none of the symbols, this is completely up to you. Using Table 1 of your Natal Chart Navigator, enter the location of each planet, degree, and sign into the appropriate house.

STEP 4:

There is something that your soul craves, a deeper want that drives your life forward—the Part of Fortune. Enter the location of your Part of Fortune from The Fortunes worksheet into the appropriate house of your Natal Chart.

STEP 5:

Right now at this very moment, Jupiter is supporting your spiritual expansion and abundance. In chapter 11 you discovered which house Jupiter is currently transiting in your chart. Remember, it takes 12 years for Jupiter to transit around your chart and it is a very powerful force to align yourself with—pay attention to its journey. Looking back to the exercise from chapter 11, enter the current house and life experience Jupiter is supporting into the blank circle below your Natal Chart called Jupiter's Gift.

STEP 6:

Saturn is providing structure to the development of your life. Through the four phases of its cycle, you are able to gain valuable information into how your life will unfold. Beneath the Natal Chart, there is a circle for Saturn's Rule. Look back to chapter 10 to determine the current phase Saturn is in for your life. Enter the phase and description into this circle. For example: Phase 1: Take Off and Climb, Phase 2: Cruising Altitude, Phase 3: Final Descent, Phase 4: Landing.

STEP 7:

It is now time to determine the three most powerful tipping point years of your life. To calculate these years, we will do the math by hand on the right side of the worksheet.

In Table 1 of your Natal Chart Navigator, determine the degree of your Natal Sun. You can enter this number into the circle in the top right box for calculations. This will be used as the "X" in the first equation. Please note, each number you calculate gets used in the following equation. Once you complete the math, the three numbers you entered represent three different years of age—these three specific ages mark the most powerful tipping point years of your life. Enter them into the blank middle circle beneath your Natal Chart.

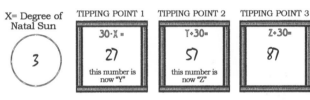

X= Degree of Natal Sun	TIPPING POINT 1	TIPPING POINT 2	TIPPING POINT 3
3	$30 \cdot X =$ 27 this number is now "Y"	$Y \cdot 30 =$ 57 this number is now "Z"	$Z \cdot 30 =$ 87

STEP 8:

It's time to claim your power and to trust your instincts. Move forward confidently and in alignment with your true spiritual purpose. IF this book moved you, please pay it forward so that more people may claim their power. Thank you from my heart for allowing me to be your guide on this spiritual journey.

In light and love, Emily

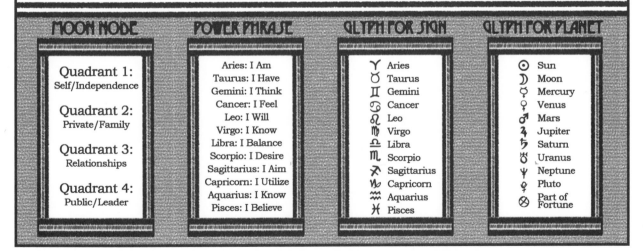

MOON NODE	POWER PHRASE	GLYPH FOR SIGN	GLYPH FOR PLANET
Quadrant 1: Self/Independence	Aries: I Am	♈ Aries	☉ Sun
	Taurus: I Have	♉ Taurus	☽ Moon
	Gemini: I Think	♊ Gemini	☿ Mercury
Quadrant 2: Private/Family	Cancer: I Feel	♋ Cancer	♀ Venus
	Leo: I Will	♌ Leo	♂ Mars
	Virgo: I Know	♍ Virgo	♃ Jupiter
Quadrant 3: Relationships	Libra: I Balance	♎ Libra	♄ Saturn
	Scorpio: I Desire	♏ Scorpio	♅ Uranus
	Sagittarius: I Aim	♐ Sagittarius	♆ Neptune
Quadrant 4: Public/Leader	Capricorn: I Utilize	♑ Capricorn	♇ Pluto
	Aquarius: I Know	♒ Aquarius	⊗ Part of Fortune
	Pisces: I Believe	♓ Pisces	

OTHER SCHIFFER BOOKS ON RELATED SUBJECTS:
Astrology of Sustainability. J. Lee Lehman, PhD. ISBN: 978-0-7643-3805-2

Pick Your Numbers! Use Tarot, Numerology, and Astrology to Play Games of Chance. Carla Smith-Willard & Clint Willard. ISBN: 978-0-7643-5260-7

The Magic of Electional Astrology. J. Lee Lehman, PhD. ISBN: 978-0-7643-4735-1

Designed by John P. Cheek
Cover design by Brenda McCallum
Cover artwork by Janet Chrysakis

Type set in Gotham/Adobe Garamond Pro

ISBN: 978-0-7643-5272-0
Printed in China

Published by Schiffer Publishing, Ltd.
4880 Lower Valley Road
Atglen, PA 19310
Phone: (610) 593-1777; Fax: (610) 593-2002
E-mail: Info@schifferbooks.com
Web: www.schifferbooks.com

For our complete selection of fine books on this and related subjects, please visit our website at www.schifferbooks.com. You may also write for a free catalog.

Schiffer Publishing's titles are available at special discounts for bulk purchases for sales promotions or premiums. Special editions, including personalized covers, corporate imprints, and excerpts, can be created in large quantities for special needs. For more information, contact the publisher.

We are always looking for people to write books on new and related subjects. If you have an idea for a book, please contact us at proposals@schifferbooks.com.